The
Perfection
of Marketing

To help anyone struggling with
their marketing find success.

The
Perfection
of Marketing

The CEO's Guide to Building a Brand
and Driving Sales in Three Steps

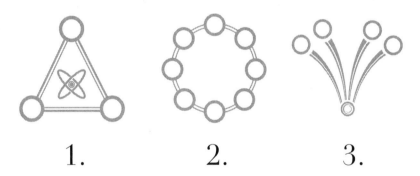

1.   2.   3.

James Connor

DIAMOND CUTTER PRESS
Pompton Plains, New Jersey

Published in 2008 by
Diamond Cutter Press
512 Newark Pompton Turnpike
Pompton Plains, NJ 07444

Website: www.diamondcutterpress.com

Printed in the United States of America

Library of Congress Cataloging-in-Publication Data is
available upon request.

ISBN 978-0-9765469-3-1

Table of Contents

The Perfection of Marketing contains the best practices of marketing in three main steps your company can logically implement for superior marketing results. This book is a conversation between a company CEO and a brand marketing expert about overcoming bad marketing habits with best practices.

Chapter 1

THE BRAND MARKETING ENGINE

Peter Gibbons sighed—the kind of sigh only losing hundreds of thousands of dollars on ineffective marketing could buy.

"I'm told you can tell me how to fix our marketing," he said leaning back in a sensible wooden chair, designed to speed meetings in the equally sensible conference room. A manila folder, contrasting with the table's mahogany, lay tattered to his left. The insides overflowed the little folder.

"That would be some of your company's marketing materials," I stated. "May I have a look?"

Quickly, spreading the materials on the table, I glanced at no less than five different ad campaigns, two website designs, four brochures, three different company logos. They were good graphic design. But that was all. Each piece lacked the key marketing techniques that make the difference between advertising expense and advertising return on investment. Collectively, nothing more than throwing things against the wall, hoping something would stick.

I smiled gently. "*Fix* implies your marketing once was working. By looking at your ads, I can tell your marketing has never made money for you or your company."

Through the silence I could see the emotion rising. "I don't get marketing," Peter began. "I've worked hard to build this company. For eight years, every day, every night—I do nothing but think about how to make it better. We work so hard." He spoke with the determination of a prize-fighter. "We're great at what we do. Our customers love us. But here's the thing. We can't quickly explain our story. We can't break through to the next level."

I nodded, understanding I was meeting yet another CEO determined to crack the marketing puzzle. For twelve years, on an almost weekly basis, I and other Brand Strategists from The James Group had met with CEOs of midsized companies. They were just like Peter, needing marketing answers to get to the next level. These meetings were interesting struggles: brand best practices sparring to overcome marketing bad habits.

"Can I use your white board?" I asked. "I want to show you something that will give us a better picture of where your company is." Opening the wooden cabinet doors revealed a white board the width of an arm span. Revenue numbers written in holiday red and green dotted the surface, along with a wish list of customer segments they hoped to reach to achieve those goals.

"You can erase that," he said matter-of-factly.

In blue pen, on the newly cleaned board, I drew three rectangles. In the center rectangle, I wrote OPERATIONS. In the right rectangle, I wrote FINANCE, purposely leaving the first rectangle blank. "Every business," I explained, "No matter what you make, who your customers are, or where you're located in the world, has three main engines of business."

I pointed to the Operations box. "Operations is where you spend most of your time, because it's what you're best at and the thing you enjoy most. You wake up knowing you have a unique perspective, a unique philosophy for how to supply something your customers want. The fact you have customers who love you, says there is a vital reason for your business to exist and that you know how to deliver your product."

Peter nodded. It was an accurate description. "So we can give you a check in this box," I said. "You have mastered operations."

"You can grade that an A," Peter said with confidence. The accomplished pride of the company founder glowed through his rugged skin.

"O.K. let's use grades and we'll give Operations an A." I put the high grade under the rectangle.

He was emphatic. "It's true. We may be among the best in the world."

"That you have been around for eight years also says that you've learned to manage your finances." I pointed to the Finance box. "Maybe it didn't start that way, but you acquired those skills or found people who had them. What should we put as a grade?"

"Let's call that one a B. It would be an A, but we're wasting money on marketing. That's hurting the bottom line."

I wrote his grade assessment under Finance. Then, drew a larger rectangle around both the Operations and Finance boxes. "Your company is flying on two of the three engines of business," I said. "This makes you a good business. Most of the businesses that survive in the world are like this. But that's also the bad news isn't it?"

I looked at Peter closely, trying to see into his mind. "You don't want to be like most of businesses in the world, do you? You just survive. Every year is a continuous struggle."

The endless responsibility of constantly having to save the day weighed on Peter's shoulders. His darting eyes displayed worry over a dozen encroaching issues. It was clear what he wanted: he wanted the business to propel itself far more.

"You're a good business," I said, again pointing at the board. "But good businesses, become great businesses when you kick in the third engine of business: Brand Marketing. I don't mean marketing tactics. That third engine is Brand Marketing." I wrote BRAND MARKETING in the left box and sat back down at the table with Peter.

"I have good news for you," I said placing my hand flat on the table for emphasis. "You've done the hard part already. Everything you need to learn about the engine of Brand Marketing, I can teach you in three logical steps. And the first step will be 70% of what you need to know."

"Really?" he responded incredulously, folding his arms.

"Sometimes I'm embarrassed by how easy my job is," I said. "You see brand positioning and advertising have been around long enough to become a mature science. There are well-documented best practices. If you just look at successful companies and think about what works in the world, you'll see marketing is really binary at this point—like a light switch. There are simple lists: do this; don't do that. Then, you are more likely to succeed.

"It's just that few people really think about marketing from a macro perspective, from a CEO's perspective. Few people think about how to bring all the best practices of marketing into a logical path any company can follow. After all, if you don't have a consistent process, how can you have consistent results? You think that way about Operations. You have to learn to think this same way about Brand Marketing."

Peter leaned forward in his chair. "And you think this way?"

"I do. What I want to talk to you about is *The Perfection of Marketing*. It's all the best practices of marketing brought together into three simple steps. Would you like me to share them with you?"

Chapter 1 Summary

There are three engines of business: Operations, Finance, and Brand Marketing. Most businesses struggle along on the first two engines. Good businesses become great when they kick in the third engine of business, Brand Marketing.

Everything you need to know about marketing can be brought together in three logical steps.

Key Questions

1. Are your marketing dollars making money for you and your business?

2. Have you spent as much time perfecting the company's Brand Marketing engine as you have Operations and Finance?

3. Do you have a consistent process for increasing sales through Brand Marketing?

Chapter 2

DISCOVERING A BRAND PROBLEM

Peter Gibbons called for his assistant, who quickly brought in a yellow legal note pad. The assistant left us alone in the room, this time closing the conference room door. The pristine condition of the room suggested very little real discussion occurred here. That was about to change.

Peter looked at his watch. "O.K., James. Tell me everything I need to know about brand marketing—in three steps. If I like what I hear in the first step, I'll listen to the other two steps."

"Fair enough," I said. "As I explain, I want you to do something."

"What's that?" Peter asked.

"Sit back and think about your business. Think how you'll do it differently once you gain a clear understanding of the steps you should take."

Peter's breathing was slowing down, already focusing his thoughts on his business. I wanted Peter to see the moment they made their first marketing mistake. It was the same point for nearly every company.

"Almost every company fails in their marketing before they even begin. They launch the business. They build the product or develop the service. Then, the next thing they think is: *We need a website. We need a brochure. We need some ads.* They think tactically instead of strategically. They forget to start with the most important questions: *What is the single idea we should own? What is our Sales Moment?*

"There are probably a dozen things that can be said of your company's product or service," I began, "but only one makes the sale. This is your Sales Moment. You see, Peter, there is just too much information in the world. Ironic—because the marketplace is primitive. If people can't quickly understand what you stand for, then you won't break through. There is just too much competition. If you tell many ideas, people will gravitate rapidly to the competitor who makes it simpler for them—who communicates one idea. To win, you have to keep it simple. Stay on your Sales Moment so people can instantly see how you fit in their world.

"*What is the single idea we should own? What is our Sales Moment?* These are strategic questions. Thinking tactically, instead of strategically, leads to all kinds of erratic behavior: the erratic marketing disease known as *Let's Try Something Else.* You hire different graphic designers for different tactics who usually 'yes' you to death. Or different ad agencies to develop flashy new campaigns. Nothing works like you want it to, so you retreat. Things get difficult. Every six months, someone develops a new idea and you try something else. All the while, wasting precious money and worse, losing time.

"This is cart before the horse marketing. Typically, this fails before it ever begins. How does it fail? One measure: it fails to bring return on investment."

Peter nodded and gave his telling sigh again. "That's what we did and are still doing, for many years now. So how do we get out of that cycle?"

I went to the white board to start the process of *The Perfection of Marketing*. At the top left in blue pen wrote, Step I: POSITIONING THE BRAND.

"Rolling out the brand consistently with marketing tactics is Step II. Peter, you and every company with ineffective marketing need to start over again at Step I: this is Positioning the Brand through your ownable Sales Moment."

"But we have a brand," Peter insisted. "A lot of people know our company's name. We've spent a lot of money getting our name out there, particularly in trade pubs."

I sat down again at the table. This was a sign of confusion over the meaning of brand. "Peter, let's talk about the three levels of branding. I know the term brand is one of the more overused and most misunderstood terms in marketing. Let's get on the same page before moving ahead."

Peter nodded, flipping to a new page in his note pad.

"There are three levels to branding," I explained. "The first level is an identifier of the manufacturer. It's simply an identifier of goods and services. This is no different than a sandal maker named Ishmael stamping his mark on sandals in the third century to say, if you like these sandals, go see Ishmael.

"The second level is a promise of customer experience.

9

Since this shampoo comes from Johnson & Johnson, I know it's going to be safe to use. It wasn't mixed in some trough out back, by some unreputable company, which could make my hair fall out. The second level is a promise of customer experience. Walk into any Starbucks in the world and you know how to behave and what to expect.

"The third level is the most subtle and the most powerful. It's a single idea that your company owns that tilts sales in your favor. For example, if I say, *Family fast food*, odds are, you're thinking…"

"McDonalds," said Peter quickly.

"Exactly. If I say, *Family entertainment*, you're thinking…"

"That would be Disney," Peter responded reaching for the water pitcher on the table.

If I say *The American soft drink that makes you smile*, you're thinking…"

"Dr. Pepper," said Peter.

"Really? That's interesting."

Peter shrugged, "I just like Dr. Pepper. What were you thinking?"

"A few years back, when speaking at a Venture Capital Summit in Madison Square Garden to about 400 VC's, I did this test: 85% of the audience was thinking Coca-Cola. Probably from the *Have a Coke and a smile* campaign. Or the cute polar bears drinking Coke that make you smile."

Nodding, Peter remembered one of the campaigns.

"But your example, Peter, makes a good point. Owning a brand position is not absolute. It simply tilts sales in your favor.

Think about it. When someone thinks *I want an American soft drink that is going to make me smile and feel happy*, a majority of people think Coke. That's a powerful Sales Moment: selling happiness in a bottle. Incredible, but that little movie in people's heads telling them a fizzy soft drink is going to make them happy, shows people exactly when they need the product. This one idea, a mere concept, tilts sales globally in Coca-Cola's favor every day.

"And say what you will, Pepsi has never figured out how to beat this idea, even when they consistently win taste tests. The brand experience and that Sales Moment may be more important than taste."

Peter sat back in his chair considering if it were true. Did owning a single idea give companies like McDonalds and Coca-Cola an edge over other businesses? I paused, deciding if the moment was right to reveal my biggest brand secret. "Let's do a thought experiment," I said.

"What do you mean?" Peter asked.

"Let's examine how the mind works. What did you have for breakfast this morning? Did the information come to you in words or pictures?"

In seconds Peter said, "Pictures. I saw a picture of a bagel with cream cheese and coffee. I didn't read the words *bagel with cream cheese* or *coffee*."

"Good. What did you wear to work yesterday?"

Peter's eyes moved back and forth. I could tell he was scanning his wardrobe in his mind. "Wow, I honestly don't remember. But I could see my mind scanning in pictures.

Saying, *No, it wasn't that shirt. Maybe that one.*"

Peter's mind was sharp and clear. "You're seeing something I gained from many years of meditating. When you slow the mind down and concentrate on how the mind works, you realize you're thinking in pictures. This has important implications for our happiness; and for successful marketing, one implication in particular."

Peter's eyes locked-in, focused to catch the marketing secret. "There is a mental image, a little movie that plays in your mind of the outcome you desire before you make any purchasing decision. If the product matches your movie's desire, you go for it. If it doesn't, you don't."

"That's what you meant by the Sales Moment," Peter exclaimed.

"Knowing what pictures in that movie of unmet desires triggered the sale is the ultimate key to Brand Marketing."

"Peter," I said after giving him a minute to chew on the last idea. "I want to talk about your business. What is the single idea that tilts sales in your favor? What is your company's Sales Moment?"

Peter's face went completely blank. He stared at the beige wallpaper with thin blue lines. After a few moments he said simply, "I'm not sure."

"Do all your sales people describe your company the same way?" I asked.

He looked out the window of the conference room into the hallway trying to picture what he knew of his sales people. "No, different sales people say different things."

"And your customers? When they explain who you are to other people, do they say the same thing?" Peter shook his head, no. The confusing clutter of messages only communicated a warning.

"Now step back. Think about what you know about the three levels of branding," I said. "An identifier of goods and services, a promise of customer experience, and at the most powerful, a single idea tilting sales in your favor. When you said you have a brand, because people know your company's name, which level of branding did you mean? Which level is your company at?"

Peter rocked in his chair, reluctant to voice his response. "We are only at level one. Neither we nor our target customers know our single idea. They don't know what our promise is. So they don't know what to expect from us. I guess our name only identifies us as the makers of the product. Not much more. And worse, I still can't say what our Sales Moment is."

Peter Gibbons had clearly diagnosed his company's problem. He gazed out the conference room window searching for an answer.

"Your company has a brand problem," I said softly. "It's that simple—nothing more and nothing less. This is the reason you can't quickly explain your company and why you can't break through to the next level. Now that we have agreement on the problem to solve, it's just about using marketing best practices to overcome marketing bad habits."

Peter returned his gaze to my smile. Both of us nodded at the clear diagnosis.

"It's an easy test really, isn't it?" I continued making sure we understood the problem. "You could ask people in your company, *What is the single idea that tilts sales in our favor?* If they can't answer, or if you get different responses, you know you have a brand problem.

"The same for your customers. Ask your customers what you stand for. If you get different answers, you know you have a brand problem.

"Peter, advertising can be expensive. You need customers to tell your story for you. Having a clear idea of what you stand for helps word of mouth. You don't really need ad dollars to explain to you what Walmart stands for or Starbucks, do you?"

Peter shook his head, no. He saw those companies owned a clear idea.

"Every company has a Sales Moment," I said to sum up. "Particularly one that has been in business for as long as you have. We just have to make the brand clearer. You were right to bring me here today," I said. "Let's talk about how to position your brand through your ownable Sales Moment."

Chapter 2 Summary

There are three levels of branding: 1) An identifier of goods and services, 2) A promise of consistent experience, 3) Owning a single idea that tilts sales in your favor. Only the third level of branding creates a competitive advantage for companies.

People think in pictures. The Sales Moment is triggered when the movie of unmet needs playing in your target customers' mind matches the promise of your product or service. The Sales Moment determines the one idea you should own.

Key Questions

1. Has your company implemented marketing tactics like brochures, websites, and ads without first identifying your Sales Moment?

2. What is your Sales Moment?

3. Does everyone in the company describe your company the same way?

4. What do your customers say you stand for?

Step I:
Positioning the Brand through the *Sales Moment*

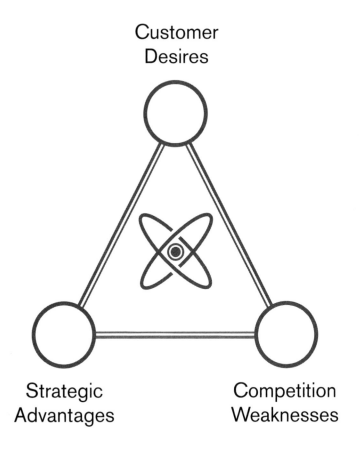

Customer
Desires

Strategic
Advantages

Competition
Weaknesses

Chapter 3

STEP I: POSITIONING THE BRAND THROUGH THE SALES MOMENT

Back at the white board, I drew three large blue circles: one circle on top and two more underneath as points in a triangle. I then connected them with three lines to finish the triangle.

"To position the brand," I said. "You have to identify your Sales Moment. This will show you the single idea that tilts sales in your favor. Notice, I keep saying *single idea*. We have to boil down all the things that can be said about your company into one idea, and one mental image, to break through the clutter."

"So how exactly do you do that?" Peter Gibbons asked, drawing the same diagram in his note pad.

"You triangulate three things to find your ownable Sales Moment." I wrote CUSTOMER DESIRES in the top circle, STRATEGIC ADVANTAGES, in the lower left circle and EXPLOITABLE WEAKNESSES OF COMPETITION in the lower right circle.

"The first thing to do is interview your customers," I said. "These people made a choice to buy from your company. They had a compelling reason to choose you over other competition. I want to know their reason. I *have* to know their reason. They will give us clear insight into your Sales Moment because they already crossed the threshold. The fastest way to double your business is to win more people who think like your current customers."

The simplicity of that strategy shined in Peter's eyes. I wanted to tell him more.

"By understanding the pattern, knowing why your customers buy, we will know which marketing messages to prioritize. By listening to what sold them, by capturing their Sales Moment, they show us how to sell other people who think just like them."

"That makes sense," Peter said.

"But whatever you do, don't do focus groups," I said. "I'll tell you frankly. Save your money. In the history of The James Group, we have never done a focus group."

"Why's that?" Peter asked

"Because people's imaginary representatives show up. They tell us how they'd like to see themselves. Not as they actually are. People tell us how they think they make decisions, not as they really do. All of the moderators' skill can't overcome the fact that people in a room full of strangers aren't speaking truthfully. It's not anyone's fault. It's just that people in a group of strangers care more about making a good first impression than letting you deep inside their mind. Remember, these people never bought. They never crossed the line to become actual customers. They are pretending, telling you about how they might buy."

"If you want the best insight, hire someone to do anonymous, one-on-one phone interviews. Choose a selection from current customers who represent the types of people that you want to do more business with in the future—your strategic wins. Tell them that you have hired an outside agency to help you understand what you can do to better serve them and better tell your story. Ask if they would be willing to participate in an anonymous 15-minute phone conversation and give their opinion."

"What if you can't reach them by phone?" Peter asked.

"No problem. Send people on-site to do one-on-one interviews with customers who volunteer. No forms. No surveys. Just conversation. People love to give their true opinion in conversation."

"That's true," Peter said.

"People also like when a company is sincerely trying to improve itself. I know I do. Don't you? Our experience is not only do we get great information, it turns into a nice public relations initiative for the company, often improving customer retention."

Peter nodded understanding how the interview process would work.

"So you can guess what we're looking for when we interview them?" I asked.

"The Sales Moment."

"Yes. We're looking for that precious key to the kingdom we call the Sales Moment. What was the little movie playing in their head right before they slid the money across the table? If we can understand that, what their unmet desires really are, we will know how to sell others who think like them. We can craft and communicate the brand to fulfill their needs. Nothing else makes the sale. People buy to fulfill a need."

"And you can get this from customer interviews?" Peter asked.

"Yes, but not directly. People aren't aware they have an unmet mental image they use to make purchasing decisions. For example, they rarely realize they are thinking, *I'm holding the future in my hand, and this will make the future easier for me,* when they buy an iPhone. But an image like this is what keeps them from buying a far cheaper cell phone and makes them leap to an iPhone. You can extract the mental image of the Sales Moment by asking the right questions.

"The questions designed for each company are different, but we might ask them, *What do you want most from this type of company? What could they do better? What did you want to get out of hiring them? What problem did they solve? What were you concerned about? What keeps you up at night?* That kind of thing. Usually no more than 8-10 questions. You just let them talk, no prompting whatsoever. You just listen."

I continued to help Peter get a clear picture. "They are talking on their phone, in an environment they feel comfortable in, anonymously. It's at a time of their choosing, and generally, they just spill information.

"The amazing thing is you don't have to listen to a lot of interviews to discover the pattern and see the Sales Moment. Some clients want us to perform at least a 100 interviews before they believe it's statistically accurate. This is because they are used to quantitative analysis.

"I'll tell you candidly though: you usually need about 10-20 customer interviews from current customers to qualitatively recognize the pattern, to see the Sales Moment clearly. Around 30, to be sure. This technique is called thin-splicing. This principal has been documented at length in Malcolm Gladwell's highly regarded book, *Blink*. About how people make a decision in a blink and how often, more information tells you less."

"So when you're done with the customer interviews, what do you do?" Peter asked.

"Nothing yet. Remember we're after the ownable Sales Moment. To find that, you have to triangulate three things. So at the same time, you're looking at the company, thinking about its strategic advantages," I said getting up and pointing to the lower left circle.

"We'll ask management, *What can you be the best in the world at? Why do you do things the way you do? What is your unique philosophy for doing business? What do you struggle with? What do you enjoy most? Looking out the next five years, who are your ideal customers?* That kind of thing."

"We recommend interviewing management one-on-one anonymously to take the politics out of the branding process and make sure all perspectives are heard. You need to be inclusive in the process because it builds consensus. We tend to share customer interview details with management as a group because it helps build consensus."

I pointed to the lower right circle. "Also, at the same time, you're looking at how your competition markets themselves. You identify what messages they are trying to own."

"We don't really have any competition," said Peter.

"Peter, you're thinking from your perspective, knowing what you know about how great your company is," I said returning to the table. "Branding is thinking from your potential customer's perspective. Standing in their shoes, making a purchasing decision in a very crowded world.

"Let's define competition as anyone your potential customer can choose as a substitute to your product or service."

"O.K," he said. "You're not judging whether it is a smart choice or not, just that a customer could choose them."

"Exactly. You make a list of your competitors and prioritize them. Then, you look closely at their marketing materials and identify what key idea they are trying to own.

"Why is that important?" Peter asked.

"Remember, you're looking for the marketing sweet spot between customer desires, strategic advantages, and the exploitable weaknesses of the competition." I cupped my hands together slowly, removing any air between them. Pulling my hands away quickly produced a loud pop.

"You're looking for the white space," I said. "You're looking for a unique ownable position."

"Tell me more," Peter said. "I'm not sure if I understand completely."

"Sometimes examples are easier. Have you heard of GarageTek?"

"Heard of them? We put a GarageTek garage in our house two months ago."

"Good. Then this story will make more sense to you. Let me guess," I said. "Your wife brought the idea to the table."

"She did," Peter responded. "How did you know?"

"We marketed it that way."

I could tell Peter wanted to know more so I explained the back-story. GarageTek was a perfect example of the best practice of positioning a brand through the Sales Moment.

"GarageTek was started in 2000 by Marc Shuman and Skip Barrett. They invented custom garage organizing systems in the U.S. These are guys' guys. They are Harley Davidson kind of guys.

"Originally, the idea was to make a cool garage to work on your bike or car in. Or to turn the garage into a functional room, since men would spend so much time working on projects in the garage. The brochures were Harley Davidson black to make it more appealing to men. They sold franchises to other guys' guys and spent a lot of time at car shows, NASCAR, that type of thing.

"After 9/11, The James Group identified *cocooning*, staying in or spending more money on the home as a trend. We cold-called GarageTek, because we thought they were doing something interesting in the home improvement space that hadn't been done before. Marc Shuman had a policy to try to meet with nearly everyone who called him, so he took the meeting. What we learned was fascinating.

"Customer sales weren't where they wanted them to be, but they knew they had a fantastic idea. Everywhere they opened a franchise, someone would start knocking off the idea, and launching a competitive product. Even Whirlpool had entered the market with Gladiator Garageworks after studying GarageTek closely.

"Now Marc Shuman is a bare-knuckle type who wasn't going to allow other competitors to steal the idea he created by under-cutting him on price with lesser product, or let a giant steam-roll him with bigger distribution and a bigger marketing budget."

Peter nodded. That was exactly the kind of tough businessman he was.

"Marc Shuman wanted to know one thing. How he could differentiate his brand and out-think his growing competition. It was a fascinating branding project for us. The stakes for GarageTek were so high.

"We found something remarkable in the customer interviews. For GarageTek, it was the woman, 75% of the time, who was bringing GarageTek to the table. She was seeing a quality in the product beyond organized, cool, or functional. She was seeing what she most wanted from a garage." Pausing, I asked Peter, "What do women most want from a garage?"

"Clean," he said without blinking. "My wife wanted it clean."

"Exactly, they want the junk off the floor, hanging on the walls behind cabinet doors, in a clean bright place they can walk through to enter their home."

"Yeah, that's why we got GarageTek."

"That's the precise Sales Moment. That's the movie or mental image that made your wife want to buy GarageTek."

"Yeah, I see it," said Peter.

"Now is it ownable?" I pointed at the Strategic Advantages circle. "GarageTek engineered a superior product for clean. The white garage panel siding they install is shiny and colored all the way through. It will never scratch or fade. Light bounces off of it making your garage brighter. The yellow sunshine strip they added at the base of their paneling as an accent on their cabinets radiates happiness. They have distinct strategic advantages."

"That's true," said Peter.

"This is why, all the marketing postcards, ads, and brochures you see are on white instead of the previous black. When you think clean, you think white.

"We realized from the customer interviews," I continued, "That we needed to position this as a home improvement decision to women, not men. After all, if you had come home and said, *Honey, lets spend $8,000 to make a really cool, functional garage*, she would say…"

"No, let's remodel the kitchen instead. My wife makes the decisions about the home."

"If you had come home and said, *Let's get the junk off the floor in the garage and install the world's cleanest garage to make our home nicer."*

"Well, she said it first."

"Exactly. From how you position the idea, what mental image you choose, you increase sales."

Peter nodded. I came and sat back down at the table.

"I believe other competitors made their mistake by relying on conventional wisdom and focus groups. If I say, *who does the garage belong to in the house,* you say..."

"The man," Peter said. "That's only because it's dark and dirty and she doesn't want to go in there."

"If I rephrase the question. Who is going to make an $8,000 home improvement decision in your home?"

"It would be made jointly."

"Good. But we both know there is no such thing as a joint decision. *So we ask who brought the idea to the table? Who was the stronger advocate?"*

"That would be my wife."

"You can't get a room full of strangers to admit that in a focus group. The moderator asks, *Who makes the decision about the garage?* The husband looks at his wife for permission, she says, *He does.* He then puffs his chest and says, *That's right, I do.* And every other couple around the table plays the same game. But you and I both know it would be a different story if you could get them anonymously on the phone, one-on-one—which is what we did."

"That's why you avoid focus groups?"

"Additionally, there is all kinds of scientific evidence which proves that when you ask people what they think about something, they are accessing the left side of their brain, which they hardly use at all for purchasing decisions. Choosing one brand over another tends to be emotionally driven, accessing the right side of the brain. Focus groups tend to negate that emotion by creating an artificial environment to ask people to analyze how they think."

"So seeing the customer desires, the product's strategic advantages, and the exploitable weaknesses of the competition—that no one was going after women for garages—the sweet spot clearly emerges," I said summing up how to position a brand. For GarageTek, the Sales Moment is *women, clean, the world's cleanest garage.*

"*The world's cleanest garage is the single idea,* the ownable Sales Moment, titling sales in GarageTek's favor every day. We were very careful to take an untrumpable brand position and trademark it, because we knew the competitors would try to imitate GarageTek as soon as they saw further success in this approach. You can't really say, *The world's more cleanest garage,* can you?

"That doesn't work," Peter said. "So did the other competitors stay with their marketing to men?" he asked.

"No. Many of them tried to imitate GarageTek, knocking off the ads nearly verbatim. But it just wasn't true. Some of the competition's products were very masculine, metallic, diamond plate, with racing stripes. Or the company was named Gladiator, which may be too masculine to appeal to women.

"Weak imitation only reinforced GarageTek as the superior choice. We already had taken the high ground of cleanest."

"So what was the result?" Peter asked.

"Three years after rolling out the new brand, under the leadership of Marketing Vice President Barbara Butensky and President Marc Shuman, GarageTek emerged as the undisputed market leader in garage organizing systems, the number one brand. They grew over three times the size of when we started with them, then expanded beyond the U.S. to license franchises in Canada and the U.K."

Peter nodded impressed with their rapid growth.

"I think they are geniuses at GarageTek. They deserve all the success they have gained from inventing the industry. Having a clearly defined Sales Moment helped them to fend off the competition and become the market leader."

"How will I know when I find my single idea?" Peter asked.

"It will be true," I said, laying my hand flatly again on the conference room table for emphasis. "True to you and your employees. True to your customers. And it will scare your competition.

"Also, you will feel it right at your heart center," I said, pointing to the center of my chest just above the solar plexus. "That little knot that has built up from not knowing how to explain who your company is in one sentence—from not knowing your Sales Moment—will just relax. It will feel like a breath of fresh air."

"I'm all for that," Peter smiled. "But tell me. Why just one idea. Isn't that a bit risky?"

"Actually, the bigger risk is not focusing," I responded quickly. "All the best companies in the world choose one central idea that they can be the best at and then they focus their marketing and operational efforts around it.

"Focus is a discipline. Those that focus, win. Those that don't focus, don't."

"But what if you do many things?" Peter asked, barely hanging on to an old idea that was never true—that being many things to many people is good business strategy.

"There is always a philosophy that unifies what you do or you wouldn't be able to do it very well," I said. "Take Virgin for example. They are good at many things, from an airline, to entertainment stores, to Virgin Bride. Behind the leadership of Richard Branson, their philosophy is clear: *if we can make it more fun, we'll do it.* That's how they unify their brand around one idea.

"Think of it like Chess. Nothing good ever happens on the board if you try to hold on to all your pieces. You have to sacrifice some very significant pieces in order to focus on winning the greater goal. Understanding your ownable Sales Moment will help you do that."

Peter sat still for a moment. He could see that focus around one brand idea was the very essence of great marketing. He could see that lack of focus around one message was holding his company back.

"So after I find my Sales Moment," he said, "what do I do?"

Chapter 3 Summary

To correctly position the brand you must identify your ownable Sales Moment. You do this by triangulating customer desires, strategic advantages, and what you can do better than your competition. Focus around one brand idea is the very essence of great marketing.

Smaller businesses defeat giants when armed with a precisely defined Sales Moment that better fulfills customers' unmet desires.

Key Questions

1. When was the last time you interviewed your customers to understand what they are looking for when they buy?

2. What can your company be the best in the world at?

3. What can you do better than your competition to truly fulfill your customers desires?

Chapter 4

THE FOUR ELEMENTS
OF A BRAND

"At its essence, a brand is a single mental image that tilts sales in your favor," I said, summing up the agreement we had come to.

Peter nodded emphatically. He could feel the power owning a single mental image or idea would bring to his business.

"Now, if you examine that mental image, you will see that it is made up of four key parts," I said writing the brand elements on the white board. "The company name, logo, tagline, and advertising campaign image.

"For example, think of Nike. What do you see?"

Peter closed his eyes. This was a good sign. He was trying to examine the mental image in his mind.

"I see that checkmark swoosh that they put everywhere," he said with his eyes still closed. "The tagline, *Just do it.* I have an image of an attractive woman in running clothes. And I can even see the lettering of their logo with the simple word *Nike.*"

"Good," I said pointing to the board and circling the elements I had just written. These were: name, logo, tagline, and campaignable image. "Very good. You see the four main elements of the mental image. These combine to communicate the brand. These four elements bring the brand to life. You can't really separate them, because from the customer's side, they are experienced nearly simultaneously."

"I didn't realize all that information was packed in there so tightly," Peter said. "But it is."

"Remarkable, isn't it?" I responded. "Can you also see how those four elements combine to communicate quite a Sales Moment? That mental image tilted sales in Nike's favor for over 20 years. Incredible aspirational power to bring out your inner athlete, before anyone else started to do that."

Peter nodded, comfortable with the brand being a sum of its parts and not one single thing.

"Here's the key to creating a powerful brand, Peter. Once you understand your Sales Moment, you make sure everything comes out of it," I said, drawing an arrow from the single brand idea to the four elements. "Particularly, these four elements, which are the foundation of your brand."

"You check to see if the company name expresses the brand idea. If not, you let it go. See if the tagline expresses the energy or philosophy of the Sales Moment. If not, you create one. See if the logo expresses the brand energy. If not, you design a new one. See if the advertising campaign image communicates the Sales Moment. If not, you change. Everything has to come from and reinforce that ownable Sales Moment to create a powerful brand."

"O.K., slow down," Peter said looking a little flustered.

"I get that these four elements combine to create my overall impression of the brand. But I'm not clear on two points. Let's start with the first. You keep saying brand idea and Sales Moment, like they are the same thing."

I paused for a moment. No CEO had called me on that. He was of course, correct. Peter Gibbons possessed an extraordinarily sharp mind. I needed go into further detail with him.

"You're right. They are different ways of saying the same thing," I said. "The brand idea gets expressed through the four brand elements that make the mental image. You saw that with the Nike example looking at name, logo, tagline, and campaignable image. That's from your side. Then, when the customer meets your brand, the mental image that the brand elements conjure triggers the Sales Moment."

"Tell me more," Peter said.

"A brand is a single idea that tilts sales in your favor. It's expressed through visual and verbal cues including the name, logo, tagline, and advertising campaign image," I said pointing at the four elements list.

1. Name
2. Logo
3. Tagline
4. Advertising Campaign

$=$ (BRAND) $\cdots$ 🙂 $=$ SALES MOMENT

Then, I drew an equal sign from the four elements to a new circle drawn in blue and labeled BRAND. Next to this brand circle, I quickly drew a person looking at the circle.

The brand triggers the Sales Moment. "Here's the magic, Peter," I said. "If you get this, you'll get the secret to brand marketing.

"The four brand elements create the mental image, which triggers the Sales Moment. The Sales Moment occurs when a person's unmet desires match up with the mental image of your brand. So the brand image and Sales Moment are two sides of the same coin; it's what you create from your side and what the customer experiences from theirs."

Peter went through it in his mind. He repeated slowly what I had told him. "That's why you just shortened it to say the brand idea is the Sales Moment. You are saying the mental image from four brand elements triggers the Sales Moment. Got it."

I was thrilled to be talking the most powerful subtleties of brand marketing with such a sharp person. "What you just caught is really important. Now, you understand the link between branding and sales. If your four elements of name, logo, tagline, and advertising image don't combine to make an ownable Sales Moment that differentiates you and matches up with someone's unmet needs, you will have a hard time triggering sales.

"This will only become more true every year," I said, "as the amount of information a person comes into contact with increases, they will have to sort things faster to determine what is relevant to their life. By focusing on the essential idea, you make it easy for them, dramatically increasing the probability of a sale."

"That explains why we can't break through to the next level, doesn't it?" Peter said. "And why the company depends so heavily on me? The current Sales Moment is just other companies trusting me and other key sales people with their needs. There is only so much of us to go around."

I nodded. He had come very far in the first thirty minutes.

I braced myself for the inevitable backsliding that would follow as the usual bad marketing habits tried to reassert themselves. These bad habits were business killers. Heavy anchors that kept a business from getting anywhere.

"But James, you're talking about Nike," Peter said. "They've spent hundreds of millions of dollars on advertising. What does that really have to do with a business like mine?"

"Learn from the best. Learn how mental images work," I said anticipating this response. "Pay attention to everything, except for the marketing spend. Nike spent millions on their marketing and brand only because they have billion dollar goals. Do you have billion dollar revenue targets or world-domination as a goal?"

"No, far from it," Peter said. "I was thinking more about how to double or triple my business in the next few years."

"Good. Then, you won't spend like them," I said. "Nike has to convince millions of people to buy their brand. How many do you need to convince?" I asked.

"Less than a hundred," Peter shrugged.

"Nike has to differentiate itself from very motivated competition with similar products that could be good substitutes in the eyes of a customer."

"That's true," Peter said.

"So they differentiate themselves, using these powerful

elements of branding to create a mental image that triggers the Sales Moment," I said.

"Peter," I said returning to the table. "You have to do the same thing. You have to use these same brand building blocks to convince a hundred or so businesses to choose you over the competition. And better yet, your competition won't be using these techniques, because they are thinking exactly like you used to. They think a midsized business like yours doesn't need to use marketing best practices. This will give you a remarkable edge."

Peter nodded in agreement. He could see the advantage again.

"Think of it this way," I continued. "You're already touching customers with your trade ads, brochures, and website. You have to have a company name, logo, tagline, and advertising image. Why not take the best practices of the greatest brands in the world and apply them to a midsized business like yours? Apply everything, but the marketing spend.

"I only used Nike as an example, because it's an example you know. It makes it easier to understand the best marketing practices. You should apply these same best practices to create your brand. And frankly, even more so—with a small marketing budget there is less room for error."

I could tell he was a little overwhelmed by the prospect of having to rethink his brand, even if someone like myself was helping him. I could see that part of him was excited, but part of him just wanted to go back to thinking about his operations and new products, the things he was good at. For Peter's business to get to the next level, a battle would have to be fought to overcome the status quo of marketing bad habits.

"Peter, if you want to go from a good business to a great business, you have to perfect the third engine of business: Brand Marketing. You can't double or triple your business by continuing to focus on your operations and managing your finances. That's not where the real break-though is going to come.

"Brand Marketing means going back to Step I: Positioning the Brand through the Sales Moment, then bringing the brand to life through the four main elements.

"Peter you have three options. You can put your head in the sand, which will achieve nothing. Keep wasting marketing dollars with various tactics producing poor results. Or you can do it right."

"Alright, what you're saying makes sense," Peter said realizing that there was no alternative.

"My other question," he said as if bracing himself. "I think you are trying to tell me something about our company name."

Chapter 4 Summary

A brand is a single mental image that tilts sales in your company's favor. It is made up of four brand elements: name, logo, tagline, and ad campaign image. From a potential customer's perspective, they are experienced nearly simultaneously.

To create a powerful brand, all four elements must quickly communicate the Sales Moment. If they don't, the brand elements create a weak mental image or send mixed messages—potentially confusing your target customer.

Businesses grow rapidly when the mental image from the four brand elements triggers the Sales Moment.

Key Questions

1. Do all four brand elements of your company or product (name, logo, tagline, and ad campaign) communicate your Sales Moment?

2. Do you feel Brand Marketing best practices are something only a large company needs?

Chapter 5

WHAT'S IN A NAME?

A wave of relief went through my body. Peter was serious about addressing the weaknesses in his company's brand. Company or product names were always a sensitive topic. I poured more water into his glass and some more for myself.

"Yes, I do have something to tell you," I said, "Though, I'm glad you said it first. Your company name, GPL International, doesn't communicate any Sales Moment."

"Sure it does," Peter said defensively. "It's my initials scrambled."

I smiled at the absurdity of his position. Over the last twelve years, I had heard many CEOs articulate positions that were detrimental to their goals. I hoped I could give Peter Gibbons a new way to look at company names.

"Why didn't you just take your initials in proper order and be PLG International," I asked in a telling manner.

"My lawyer said someone in the state had already registered a corporation named PLG, so we just went with GPL," he said.

"And you expect potential customers to be able to tell the difference between PLG and GPL?" I asked bearing in.

Peter sat blankly.

"And what brand idea or mental image does GPL communicate?" I asked. "Are you telling me that people recognizing your initials scrambled is the Sales Moment that fulfills your customers' unmet needs?"

"I guess not," Peter said. Peter could see the truth of the situation, but he was still reluctant to face it. "You forgot the International," he said. "We are international."

"Isn't everybody these days?" I responded. "Are you telling me that being international is the single mental image that tilts sales in your favor? Or that it is the thing that you can do better than your competition?" I asked.

Peter shook his head a reluctant no.

"Worse, if you have to say it, it's almost like, it's not true," I added.

"But what about IBM or AT&T?" he said. "Those are great companies. And they are initials."

In that moment, I understood exactly what had happened. Peter Gibbons had crashed on the reef of three-letter naming. It was the single worst mistake in company naming.

"If you can get in a time-machine, go back to the 1920's, and set-up a quasi-governmental monopoly, you can name your company anything you want." I responded emphatically.

"Consider the last decade. In an infinitely more competitive marketplace, can you name any new initial designated companies that have become category leading brands?" I asked.

Peter took several minutes. He really didn't want to concede this point. You could almost see smoke coming from his ears.

"There's Fedex," he said. "It was abbreviated from Federal Express."

"Yes," I said. "It's a great, proprietary brand name, created from the morphemes of Federal Express. But an abbreviation is not an acronym, is it?"

He shook his head no. He kept trying to think of companies with three initials. Then, finally, after valiant effort, gave up.

"I can't think of any," he said. "But that doesn't mean there aren't any."

"True," I said. "I can't think of any either. Instead, many new brands come to mind that have become category leaders in the last decade that are not three initial companies. Their names create stronger mental images. Some of them even have cut dramatically into IBM's and AT&T's market share."

Peter nodded realizing this was true.

"Besides the point that three letter names make weak mental images and don't communicate a Sales Moment," I continued, "remember the main reason why initials were used in the first place. The companies you mentioned are old companies that invented industries. In the old days, before countless brands were created, branding could be done simply by product description. Later the product lines these companies were named after became anachronistic. They had to change. Can we expect a person on the West Coast to buy a cell phone or Internet Broadband from Atlantic Telephone & Telegraph?" I asked.

"I guess not," Peter responded.

"Nobody thinks of computer chips or technology consulting

as being an International Business Machine," I continued. "Think of CTS, Chicago Telephone Supply. After 110 years of business, they now supply high-tech O-rings to the Space Shuttle and electronic components like the little red-knobbed navigation stick on laptops. They are no longer just supplying telephones to Chicago."

Even after explaining the errors in naming his company after scrambled initials, Peter was unconvinced.

"But you named your company, The James Group," he said, "What about that?"

I sat back. This was a distraction to avoid truly facing the weakness of his company's name. I thought about how to help him. He was frustrated by the implications of change. Understanding that he wasn't alone in facing major brand change would help.

"I'll tell you a few stories," I said, in a more relaxed tone.

"For 15 years, Phil Knight operated *Blue Ribbon Sports*, with the checkmark swoosh that you know today. It was a good company with a tremendous logo. The company name changed to *Nike* in 1981. Phil Knight wisely started working with advertising guru, Dan Wieden in 1982. The Nike name came from the Greek Olympic chant meaning 'win, win, win.' When this less pedestrian, edgier name combined with that great tagline, *Just do it* and those incredible athletic images, the company finally took off."

"I didn't know Nike was the Blue Ribbon Sports for 15 years," Peter said taken aback.

"Why would you?" I responded. "It wasn't a very good

name. Similarly, one of the names considered for the greatest coffee franchise in the world was *Pequod Coffee*."

"Pee what?" Peter said.

"The owners loved Melville's *Moby Dick*. One of the founders was an English professor. As I understand it, they wanted this nautical theme, which also made sense in Seattle, where they began. That's why there is a mermaid on the side of the cup you know. They considered naming it, Pequod, after the ship in *Moby Dick*. Can you imagine Pequod Coffee taking over the world? What mental association do you have between coffee and Pequod?"

"An uncomfortable one that makes me want to go to the bathroom," Peter laughed.

"Thank God someone intervened and said something like, O.K., we can work with this Moby Dick theme, but how about going with the first mate's name, Starbuck. At least people can spell that and it seems to better convey the Sales Moment of premium coffee you would pay big dollars for."

"So you're saying I'm more likely to go to Starbucks than Pequod?" Peter asked.

"Martha Stewart's birth name is Martha Kostyra," I responded. "Is a person more likely to want to read *Martha Kostyra Living* or *Martha Stewart Living*?"

"Martha Stewart," Peter said.

"Why?" I asked.

"I don't know. I guess it sounds more high-end. Less old-world refugee," Peter shrugged.

"So you're saying it conjures different mental images.

Is that fair?" I asked.

"No," he said. "It's just how it works."

"You see, branding isn't fair, it just functions. What we name things is important. It sends verbal cues that create mental images."

Peter nodded seeing how names contribute to the overall mental image of the brand. But I still had to answer his original question. "You asked why we are called The James Group. People choose advertising agencies primarily on whose philosophy they trust. This is why historically, great agencies have been named after the last names of the principles, for example, Ogilvy from advertising innovator, David Ogilvy, or the famous agency, Saatchi & Saatchi. Now my last name is Connor. In the history of the world, there hasn't been a successful Irish advertiser."

Peter laughed.

"If I was opening Connor's pub in New York City, there would be a line around the door," I mused.

"So instead of fighting against an unfair common mental image my last name could convey, I used my first name instead, James. James is more English and more in the tradition of the great English companies who refined the science of branding. Additionally, in America, you hear The James Group and you may think, The James Gang. Gunslingers. Like we're the Navy SEALS of branding. If there is a brand problem we drop in and solve it.

"We play on that with our aggressive brand promise in our tagline, *Our clients make more money*™."

"That certainly gets to the point," Peter said. "Making more money would be the only reason I'd hire you."

"It's the only reason you should," I responded. "So you see, Peter, you've described your Sales Moment for hiring an advertising agency. You're looking for an advertising agency that is so good at their craft, and so fast, they can out-maneuver your competition before they can even respond and make you more money. That's what you want more than the image of a drinking buddy. Isn't it?"

"O.K. I'm convinced," he said. "If we changed our name, how would we go about it?"

The hard fight was done. But there was still more to establish to keep him from backing away from a change that could prove pivotal in achieving his company's success.

"I'll explain how to develop a powerful name in a moment, but the most important thing is this," I said summing up. "There is only one reason to change a company name. If you think, by doing so, you can make more money. That's the only reason."

There was a palpable silence in the room, then Peter nodded. "So you don't change every company's name you work with?" he asked.

"Of course not," I answered. "Only if it will help them significantly. Historically, this has occurred in about a fifth of our brand repositionings.

"The majority of the time, the current name communicates brilliantly; or the name is close enough to the brand idea that you leave it alone and let other brand elements do the heavy lifting; or the brand equity is too great to change. If the ability of the new name to more clearly signal the Sales Moment you want to own outweighs the current equity in the brand name, then you change the name. The new name creates a more powerful mental image. The purpose of branding is to own a mental image. This is why you make more money by changing the name."

"That makes sense," Peter said. I could see there was still something troubling him. I knew exactly what it was. He would put his finger on it, if I just sat quietly for a moment.

"But how do you announce the name change?" He asked. "Won't people think there is something wrong with my company that is forcing us to change the name?"

Peter Gibbons had hit on his final worry. The fear that could keep him from making a brand marketing breakthrough. "You have to handle it right, but I've only seen it be a positive," I answered, pleased to have an opportunity to address this question.

"Think about how cluttered the marketplace is, Peter. For you, a name change will be a great time to focus attention and new interest on your company and articulate what you stand for. You've never really told the marketplace what you stand for."

I could tell he agreed with the opportunity, but he was getting stuck on how to operationalize the name change.

"Here's what you do exactly," I said clearly explaining the game plan The James Group had used so effectively in so many cases in the past. "You explain the new brand to your employees first, using the new advertising creative and highlights from the brand findings, so they are comfortable and prepared to answer any questions they receive.

"Second, you tell your current customers. We usually do this with a letter on the new stationery with an ad slick. The letter explains that after doing interviews with your customers, you learned the key reason why customers choose you. The letter says you changed the company name to better reflect your unique positioning. They can expect the same commitment to great service. The letter also explains how the name was derived. Then, the ad shows them the new brand in its entirety, demonstrating how the new brand comes to life. This will often lead to referrals to help you move forward with your new brand.

"Third, after current customers have been informed, you run ads announcing the name change and new brand to your target marketplace. This tells people who heard about you before, but didn't buy, that they need to take another look."

"Alright," Peter said getting excited for the first time since we had begun the naming discussion. "I can see how that would be a cost-effective way to generate buzz and get people looking at us again. And I see how in the long-term a new name would better help us to own an idea.

"How do you come up with names?" He asked. "Do you just sit around and brainstorm ideas?"

"Peter," I said, "There is a process for everything."

Chapter 5 Summary

Company brand names should reflect the Sales Moment and help you own a mental image. What we call things is important: the label creates mental images that influence the sale.

Three-letter naming, following the example of IBM and AT&T, is the single worst mistake in company naming. Those giants were quasi-governmental monopolies from the early 1900's. In the cluttered contemporary marketplace, three-letter names create weak mental images. As initials do not convey a Sales Moment, this makes acronym naming a poor choice.

There is only one reason to change a company name. If by doing so, you can make more money.

In a cluttered market place, a name change often provides a great opportunity to focus attention and new interest on a company to articulate what the company stands for.

Name change announcements have to be handled skillfully and there is a clear process for doing so to maximize marketing results.

Key Questions

1. On its own, what mental image does your company name convey?

2. Does this mental image convey your company's Sales Moment?

Chapter 6

HOW TO CREATE
A POWERFUL BRAND NAME

"There are six types of naming to consider in creating a powerful brand name," I said going back to the white board. "I'll show you how it's done. But most importantly, remember the name has to come out of the Sales Moment you want to own to create the most powerful brand results.

"If you already had a famous brand name, or a brand name that created a strong mental image that was strategic to own, we would skip this step. But in your case…"

"I know," Peter said. "I don't have a company name that creates a strong mental image or is famous. Keep going."

"I also don't want you to jump to creative solutions today, because we haven't done the customer interviews, management interviews, or competitive research to identify your ownable Sales Moment. This is only to describe the naming process."

"That makes sense," Peter said. "Idea first. Then check to see if your name supports it. If not, create a new brand name."

"Well said." On the white board, I wrote: NAMING TYPES: FUNCTIONAL, METAPHOR, ENERGY, MORPHEME, HISTORIC, FAMILY.

"Functional naming," I began, "is naming after a key product feature that you want to own. The name functions for what it does. For example, a liquid you can use to unclog a drain instead of calling a plumber becomes *Liquid Plumber*. It's a great brand name that owns the Sales Moment. Somebody is standing over a clogged drain, thinking, *I wish there was something I could pour into the drain to unclog it, before I have to spend more money on a plumber.* Then the image comes to mind, *I need Liquid Plumber.* That name is genius, because it captures the Sales Moment and tilts sales in their favor."

"You know exactly what you are buying and why," Peter stated.

"Exactly. You caught the essence of Functional naming. Some functional names are a little less obvious, but equally remarkable. Consider how the cotton circle at the end of a stick becomes a Q-Tip. It looks like the letter 'Q,' the cleaning stick functions with a Q-Tip, so they named it that way."

"So, I should consider choosing a Functional name for my company?" Peter asked impatiently.

"You should consider all six types of naming. Every branding choice also contains a weakness. Functional names are clear and extremely useful depending upon your strategy. But sometimes, Functional names tend to signal a lower price point. You have to be careful with your other brand elements, so the company doesn't appear cheap or unsophisticated compared to other brands."

"Can you give me an example?" Peter asked.

"Well, consider *American Airlines* or *U.S. Airways*. These are functional names. So is *Southwest Airlines*. But *Southwest Airlines* did more to keep their brand vibrant, so they are less at risk of being beaten for mindshare by U.S. Airways or American Airlines."

"Got it. You're quick with examples, James."

"Comes from seeing the world through the lens of branding. I'm always thinking about mental images, asking, *What idea is someone trying to own? Are they doing it effectively?* Maybe, I'm a little compulsive about it, but it sure helps with my job."

"I'm that way with operations," Peter said. "My wife gets so embarrassed. Everywhere we go, I tell people how they could do their job better."

"That's the CEO's curse isn't it? You always want to help people be better."

We both smiled, knowing we had similar dispositions. Meeting a peer, cut from the same cloth, carrying the same weight of executive responsibility, has its own comforts.

"Tell me about Metaphor naming?" he asked, looking at the list on the white board.

"It's using a word to suggest the key value of your brand." I emphasized the words *key value.* "For example, the world's largest online store becomes *Amazon* to convey size. Delta's new airline for happy people becomes *Song* to convey a euphoric feeling. An asset-management company specializing in fundamental indexing becomes *TransparentValue* to convey a safer, clearer way to invest your money. Or a fresh, new take on an old industry becomes *Virgin.*"

"I think I'd like to use a metaphor to name my company," Peter stated.

"Let me tell you about Energy naming," I said ignoring his last comment. "This is using words that convey the emotion, action, or tone of the brand. A great example would be *Yahoo!*"

"How's it different from Metaphor naming?" Peter asked.

"Metaphor concentrates on a key strategic value. Energy naming uses emotion or tone.

"Another example of Energy naming would be the famous children's clothing line, *OshKosh B'Gosh.* Consider how great this brand name is. The name was created in 1895, after the Wisconsin town of the company's founding. But that doesn't explain why the brand has endured for over 100 years and spread to more than 50 countries around the world, does it? That brand name has survived different management teams, countless product changes, and market changes. Still, the tone of the name matches the Sales Moment. OshKosh B'Gosh is just fun to say isn't it? So it feels like the clothes would be fun for your kids to wear. And that's what any parent or child wants."

"Sure. My little girl could say OshKosh B'Gosh before she could even read. It's Dr. Seuss-ish, isn't it?"

I nodded in agreement. "Then, there is Morpheme naming. A morpheme is the small syllable of a word that conveys essential meaning. You put these morphemes together to coin a new word. This is how *FedEx*, you mentioned earlier, was derived. Just from Fed, you recognize Federal and the 'Ex' comes from Express. Similarly, you know 'soft' signals software. And 'micro' signals personal. So *Microsoft* becomes a great brand name. *Verizon* is another example of Morpheme naming. It sounds and looks like 'horizon' which makes it big. The 'veri' is from the Latin root for 'truth' or 'true.' You recognize that on some level, suggesting Verizon is a big company you can count on for consistent phone service anywhere."

"I really like that kind of naming. Let's use that one for my company," Peter said.

In his excitement of learning new branding skills, Peter was still jumping to creative conclusions before starting at step one. I felt I better give him a top-line overview of the whole process before continuing in greater detail.

"Here's the short-hand of the naming process, Peter. Once you have a clear brand idea to spring from, and not before, develop names in all six areas. You'll then be able to determine which type of name helps you best own your brand idea. Then do trademark searches on the best naming candidates to see what is available for a federal trademark. For initial searches, you can use the USPTO database at www.uspto.gov. From what is available for trademark, choose the name that is most memorable and best owns your strategic idea. You then have a qualified trademark attorney screen your name for any conflicts. In general, you will be fine as long as you're not stepping on a famous trademark or a name that is already being used in your category of business. But please be very careful to insure your name is available for trademark."

Peter repeated back the process as he wrote it down in his

notepad. "Notice, Peter," I cautioned, "I didn't say, choose the name you like best or others like best."

"Oh come on, James," Peter said. "You're telling me I don't have to like my company name?"

This was a very sensitive issue. I had to give it to him straight. I took my seat again at the table. Inside, I wanted to shake him, so he would remember clearly what I was about to say. "Yes. That's what I'm telling you. The tests are: which is most memorable and which best owns your Sales Moment. Peter, I'm trying to save you from falling into a deadly trap.

"Executives make branding mistakes all the time by rejecting the very idea that could help their company breakthrough the clutter. They reject it with the words, *I don't like it*. Their ego has entered the discussion, blinding them from best practices. Instead, they are making decisions solely from their limited perspective of what they are comfortable with, cutting themselves off from a whole ocean of potential. Better to make the decision from the customer's perspective. What communicates the Sales Moment to the customer in a memorable way."

Peter nodded. He had seen this occur many times in his career with other companies and perhaps even with his own.

"I'll tell you plainly. If you're completely comfortable with the new creative for your brand, it's a clue—it's not good enough. It has to create a new mental image and break through the clutter. You have to lean to the side of being slightly disruptive to get people's attention."

Peter shifted in his chair.

"The marketing you're comfortable with created the situation you're in. Why repeat it? So how will you decide what to do, when you're a little uncomfortable with your new brand? Simple: reject something on the basis that it doesn't follow branding best practices, rather than subjective judgments. Why? Best practices give you the best chance of success and are the best predictors of the future. We both have to remember, we're not the customer. After all, how much stuff are you going to buy from your company?"

"Not enough," Peter responded.

"So we can't brand the company for you, me, or your friends using some inside meaning that is only relevant to us. Your customer doesn't share our unique perspective. We can't choose the company color based on what we like. Instead, choose the branding elements of name, logo, tagline, and campaignable image based on what performs. Create an ownable mental image. Whether we like it doesn't really matter. What matters is the brand makes it easy for the customer to understand how it is relevant to them. That will increase sales."

Peter sat quietly for a few moments, sizing up what I had just told him. "Can you give me an example where the naming has been too internally focused?" he asked.

"You mean other than GPL International?" I said smiling.

"Other than my company."

This was an important moment. I could move Peter beyond any habit to hang on to a miserable brand name with the right example. "It happens all the time. Internally focused naming is one of the more common naming mistakes," I began. "A few years back, we rebranded a toy company with exceptionally great products. They had been in business for 18 years and were in over 40 countries. This is a successful company by anyone's standards. They make this mind challenging game, *Rush Hour.* You try to get a red car out of increasingly more complicated traffic jams. Have you seen it?"

"My little girl isn't old enough for that kind of game yet, but it sounds interesting." Peter said.

"It's kind of a three-dimensional action twist on the traditional slider puzzle. It's sold over 4 million units worldwide. So it's a major hit. They followed it up with other great games like *River Crossing* and *Gordian's Knot.*"

"So what was the problem?" Peter asked.

In 2002, sales had plateaued. Specialty toy stores were consolidating or going out of business as the big box retailers started to take over. Their distribution channels were shrinking. They weren't sure how to get to the next level. They were diversifying their product line as a possible business solution, but they weren't gaining much traction.

"We assessed the situation as mainly a brand problem. Specifically, they weren't communicating what made them unique and this would be essential to opening new channels of distribution. Back in 1985, they had named the company Binary Arts, as a play on the founders' names, Bill and Andrea. Let me ask you, does Binary Arts sound like a toy company?"

Peter shook his head. "It sounds more like a software company. Do they make software?"

"No," I responded. "That was the thing. Our customer

interviews revealed that they were regarded as the best in the industry for creating three-dimensional, hands-on, mind challenging games that everyone loved to play. They were simply the best in the world at mind challenging games, so the name had to come out of that. We renamed the company, *ThinkFun*, with the tagline, *Everybody Plays*™.

"What do you think? Are you more interested in buying ThinkFun for your little girl or Binary Arts?"

"No question," Peter responded instantly. "ThinkFun sounds more like a toy company that's making fun, educational games my little girl would like and my wife would approve of. So that one."

"You just described the Sales Moment perfectly, Peter." I said, pleased again he was wielding the Sales Moment so well. "ThinkFun is an example of Functional naming expressing the key product feature they wanted to own."

"So what happened?" he asked.

"Together, we reintroduced the brand at the 100th Anniversary of Toy Fair. Bill Ritchie and Andrea Barthello were successful at convincing Barnes & Noble CEO, Steve Riggio that he had smart customers that matched their smart product. In 2004, Steve Riggio launched several strategic initiatives including putting a ThinkFun Center in nearly every Barnes & Noble in the country."

"I bet they were thrilled."

"Sure. But here's the thing. Bill and Andrea had the courage to change. They accurately assessed that market conditions were different and they would have to do something new to stand out. They deserve their success. Sometimes making a change is the hardest thing to do."

"Do you like all the names or brands you create?" Peter asked, turning an earlier question to me.

"That's not even one of the tests, is it?" I trailed off, looking out the conference room window, hoping… hoping he had caught a vital principle in creating brands.

"Most of the time, you're not the target customer," Peter said with a hint of conviction. "Better to rely on best practices."

"Good. Very good."

"I'm going to have to chew on that one for a while."

"We all do." I said. "It's only about what makes things easier for the customer. Seeing a brand The James Group created make more money for a client, and seeing the owners excited about their business' future is infinitely more satisfying than indulging personal likes or dislikes."

I was starting to get concerned about the time. I enjoyed the discussion, but I had yet to teach him one of the most important best practices: the four types of advertising campaigns that both build brand and create sales. That best practice could really help his business.

"Let me finish the last two types of naming quickly," I said. "Historic naming is using an historic character, event, or location to embody a brand. There's *Rembrant* toothpaste for a brilliant smile. *Con Edison* electric to keep your lights on, named after the inventor of the light bulb. *Baby Einstein* products to make your baby smarter."

"That reminds me, James, earlier you said, Oshkosh is a

location. So wouldn't that be an Historic type of naming instead of Energy naming?"

"By now, you can see that sometimes names overlap the different techniques used to create them. Yes, Oshkosh is a location, but they must have recognized how fun it was to say, which is why they extended the brand name to *Oshkosh B'Gosh*. That's why I grouped it in Energy naming.

"And finally, there is using a Family name. *Casio* was named this way after its great Korean founders. Same with *Samsung*. *Ford* after Henry Ford. *McDonalds* comes from the McDonald brothers Ray Kroc bought the business concept from. You just have to make sure you have a family name that is easy to spell and creates a positive mental image. And the name doesn't always have to be real. The name *Tommy Bahama* embodies the island lifestyle clothes and accessories the company sells and Tommy Bahama is a fictional person.

"Now you understand the process used to create names, but there are additional factors to consider before selecting the right name. Generally, shorter names are better: easier to remember, easier to spell. Try to avoid names that have pronunciation problems that make them difficult to say or unclear what the proper pronunciation is. If the brand is going international, you particularly have to do international language checks to avoid *Chevy Nova* problems. Nova is close to 'no go' in Spanish and I'm certain that's not a quality Latin America is looking for in a car."

"Have you ever kept a brand using a real family name? It doesn't really signal a Sales Moment?" Peter asked.

"Sure we have. Sometimes, it's the best solution. You want to pay attention to what your competition is doing. You want to zig where others are zagging.

"Let me give you an example. We recently had a high-end lawn care franchise to rebrand. They were originally called *GrassRoots*, which was clever, but not in line with their lawn care science degrees, highly developed processes, or high-end price point. The competitive research showed that most of their competition used Metaphor naming. Names like *Majestic Lawn Care*, *Regal Lawn Care*, *Augusta Lawn Care*, or *Fairway Lawn Care* that were hard to differentiate from each other in terms of mental image. So we recommended calling them *Teed & Brown*. It was family naming after Peter Teed and Chris Brown, the company founders."

"Teed & Brown sounds more high-end than GrassRoots," Peter said.

"Exactly. *Teed* also evokes the image of a golf green and you would have to be damn good to name a lawn care company with *Brown* in it. Its quirkiness makes it memorable as well. They got fewer phone calls from people that were price shopping and more business from the expensive homes that could afford custom lawn care services. So even real family names can convey a Sales Moment, right?

"The key thing about naming is this," I said to sum up. "Does the name convey the Sales Moment? Is it easy to remember? Give yourself an easy to remember, strategic name and you will win more new business. It's that simple."

Peter nodded in agreement. I could see he would give up

his initial branding for something better. "Now let's talk about your logo," I said.

Chapter 6 Summary

There are six types of naming to consider in creating a powerful brand name: Functional, Metaphor, Energy, Morpheme, Historic, and Family.

1. Functional naming uses a key product feature that you want to own.

2. Metaphor naming uses a word that suggests the key value of your brand.

3. Energy naming uses words that convey the emotion, action, or tone of the brand.

4. Morpheme naming uses the small syllables of a word to convey essential meaning.

5. Historic naming uses an historic, character, event, or location to embody a brand.

6. Family naming uses fictional or real names, usually from the founders.

Pay careful attention to make sure your name is available for Federal Trademark. Initial searches can be done through the U.S. Patent and Trademark Office database at www.uspto.gov.

Avoid choosing a name based on what you like. Choose the brand name from your customers' perspective.

Choose the name that is most memorable and which best communicates the Sales Moment.

Key Questions

1. Did you check to make certain your name is available for Federal Trademark?

2. From your customer's perspective, does the name convey the Sales Moment and is it memorable?

Chapter 7

WHAT GREAT LOGOS HAVE IN COMMON

It actually hurt to look at the logo on his brochure cover. In bold serif lettering were the words, GPL International, under a world globe. An arrow spun around the globe. I had seen generic logos like these many times before. They lacked imagination—the most likely result from not identifying a clearly ownable Sales Moment before designing the logo.

There was nothing proprietary there. Nothing ownable. The story it told would be confused with other companies. Simply forgotten. Perhaps not surprisingly, the logo was a shabby IBM meets AT&T knockoff. Worse, the literal globe looked like PowerPoint clip art used for a front company in a mobster B-movie. A sickening knot tightened in my stomach thinking about how much business Peter Gibbons had lost due to something as innocuous as this poorly designed logo.

Peter chewed on his top lip. I could see him thinking again about the time and money he had wasted. Maybe even avoiding the issue of the logo altogether.

"Please don't feel bad about anything you've done to date,"

I said. "Nobody trained you in brand marketing before. Your expertise is in creating and running this business. Remember, that's the hard part. Marketing is easy, if you just stick to best practices.

"We'll keep talking about brand best practices," I said. "Then it will be clear what has to be done to get your company to the next level. Remember why we are here today."

Peter sighed again and flipped to a new page in his notebook.

"Simplicity is the key to a great logo," I explained. "Not for simplicity's sake. Simplicity's purpose is to make it memorable. Customers can reconstruct a simple logo easily in their mind, making a clearer, more powerful mental image. The stronger the mental image, the more likely they are to remember and choose you."

Peter crossed his arms. I was going to have to overcome some resistance. The best way to do it would be by building on agreement we had reached earlier.

Outside the conference room, a tall, charismatic man wearing a finely tailored shirt passed by, quickly peering through the conference room window for the second time in the last five minutes.

"Think about the Nike swoosh," I said, choosing an earlier example that resonated well with Peter. "It says *performance, speed,* and *excellence,* in one simple gesture. Now think about the Adidas mark. It's good, but it gets beaten by the Nike swoosh, every day of the week."

"To tell you the truth," Peter said. "I can't even recall the

Adidas logo."

I reminded him it was three simple stripes leaning to the left.

"I guess I like the energy of the Nike mark better," Peter shrugged. "There is more of a story there."

"That's just it, isn't it? You've hit on an important characteristic of great logos. A logo should tell a story."

"But our logo tells a story about us being international," Peter insisted.

There it was, the thing that kept bugging him—the prospect of having to change, yet again. "True," I responded gently. "Let's see if great logos are more than just story.

"When we're evaluating or designing a logo, we look for four qualities. These four qualities are consistent with the great logos in the world. A logo should: be simple in a symbolic way, be easy to remember, differentiate from the competition, and tell a story."

Peter shifted in his chair.

"When we have a clearer understanding of logo best practices, we can talk further about your logo." I said, buying time until Peter would be able to see his logo's weaknesses for himself. "You remember the Nike logo more than the Adidas logo…"

"Sure."

"Let's test our four guidelines of logo qualities on why you remember the Nike logo more than Adidas. The Adidas logo certainly passes the test for simplicity and differentiation. Do you agree?"

"I guess," Peter responded reluctantly.

"But what story do the three stripes tell you? What does it symbolize?" I asked.

Peter shrugged. He wasn't sure. "I've got nothing."

"It's unclear, isn't it? Which is why it's not as memorable to you." I said. "You're not attaching a mental image or story to it."

"So you would advise them to change it?" Peter asked.

"Not at this point. It's a reasonably famous mark and they even have an older vintage logo that they still place on some of their products. The one that kind of resembles a marijuana leaf. Adidas can use other brand elements like its ad campaign or tagline to make the brand more memorable."

"So I don't have to change my logo, either? I mean we could change the name, but at least try to keep the logo idea. Maybe as a transition."

This was proving more difficult than I had expected. "Think about other great logos you admire," I continued trying to reach a deeper understanding.

"Well, I drive a Lexus. They have such a great commitment to quality engineering," Peter said. "They also have a great logo."

"True," I responded, noting that he recalled Lexus through the single idea that tilted sales in their favor. "Elegant, sophisticated, reinforcing the brand 'L' in a stylized way that feels like driving on an open road."

"But I guess the Mercedes logo is the most famous car logo," Peter said.

"And what do you see in that logo?"

"It's such a symbol. I just think Mercedes," Peter said. "It shines like a star for me. But I think it's supposed to be a steering wheel."

Now we were getting somewhere. "That's what I mean by simple in a symbolic way," I said. "The logo shouldn't be literal. It should be more symbolic. You see, Peter, symbols have primitive power. You want to tap into that power to create a logo. If it is too literal, people stop looking. It will lack symbolic power.

"Can you imagine if the Mercedes logo were an actual steering wheel with a car horn button and everything?" I asked.

"People wouldn't want that on hats or key chains," Peter mused. I could see him opening up again, picturing a literal steering wheel logo, maybe even in magazine ads. "It would be ridiculous and like you said, less powerful."

"Like your literal globe?"

The light was beginning to shine for Peter. He flipped to a new page in his yellow legal pad and made a quick note. "So we could stylize the globe in some way to make it simpler and more unique?" He asked.

"You could do that," I responded. "That would be better. But it probably still won't get you where you need to be."

Peter looked confused.

"We talked about being simple in a symbolic way. You understood that. We talked a little about telling a story. Now think of how many globe logos with arrows there are in the world."

"I can't think of any," Peter responded quickly.

"You see them and ignore them all the time because there isn't anything unique about them, anything proprietary. They don't differentiate. It's very difficult for those logos to create strong, ownable mental images. Therefore, you can't remember them.

"In contrast, think about the Apple logo," I said, choosing another example to bring the issue of differentiation to life. "Think about how revolutionary it was to create a personal computer in 1976 and put a six-color, rainbow Apple on that machine. Nearly everything at the time was government-centric big blue. It clearly said this was something different. It was a personal computer for the home—a family computer. This was a happy source of knowledge. That simple name and radically different logo, helped clearly define a market segment for Apple. Their identity helped them cut through the clutter, and become one of the major players in computing."

"But they did get beat by Microsoft," Peter said using a common criticism of Apple.

"You could argue that Apple made a strategic mistake in not licensing their operating system before Microsoft—in not sharing their great product with more people. But I'm sure nobody is crying for Apple. Remember this is a company that keeps gaining market share and posting record profits. They are the market leader for MP3 players with the iPod, music downloads with iTunes, and with the iPhone, you'd have to say the future looks bright for Apple. On some level, they must have understood their earlier misstep. They have been very proactive in nurturing a whole secondary market allowing other companies to create accessories for the iPod, helping other companies to succeed too.

"Apple understands their brand is about making complex technologies easy and sexy. You can see that with their new products. It makes sense that they dropped the six colors from their logo, and usually have it in knockout white. It's simpler. Now they look more like a fashionable lifestyle company."

"They do have great packaging," Peter commented. "I can see the Apple logo as clearly as the Nike swoosh."

"And memorability is one of the key factors that make a great logo."

I walked Peter briefly through a few additional guidelines he would need to consider. How to make sure the company name was legible. How, typically, we used a trademark and stylized word mark combined to bring the identity to life. The importance of the logo working in black and white as well as in color. How we tested the logo by applying it to a variety of tactics like ad mockups, packaging, or signage at various sizes to make certain it worked in the real world, before making a final logo recommendation. How, most importantly, you needed to test the logo by seeing if you could recreate it easily in your mind for a strong mental image.

"Don't take short-cuts with your logo," I added. "Company logos are attached to millions of dollars of revenue. I'm amazed by companies that aren't willing to spend a few thousand dollars to have professional brand designers, who are trained in the science of identity development, create their logo.

"Perhaps these companies think graphic designers and

brand designers are the same thing. After all, they both use the same design programs on the computer. But in my experience, graphic designers and brand designers look at the world very differently. Their thinking is different; the results of their work are different too. Graphic designers tend to try to solve a design challenge in a cool way. Brand designers tend to try to own a strategic idea. In my experience, only one approach can consistently help your business."

Peter nodded. "We didn't use anything like your four logo principles when we created our logo. And the graphic designers we hired, unfortunately never talked to us about communicating the Sales Moment through our brand. To tell you the truth, I never really liked the logo anyway. We just couldn't come up with anything better."

"There's a key reason why you didn't come up with a more brandable logo. You said it earlier and I found it interesting."

"What was that?"

"You said your logo tells a story of you being international. But I remember earlier you conceded that this wasn't the idea that tilts sales in your favor."

"Yeah that's true. I did say that."

"So you see, the logo creation was doomed before it began—because it wasn't designed around an ownable brand idea. The real benefit of repositioning the brand all at once is synergy. Synergy between the Sales Moment you want to own and the name, logo, tagline, and campaignable image. All creating a vastly more powerful brand."

Peter grimaced—deep acknowledgement that his company

had made a mistake thinking of these things as separate elements and not a synergistic mental image.

"You have to let go of the idea that you don't need to look like a big company. You don't have to settle. Perception becomes reality. Use the same best practices. If your logo doesn't match up to the great brands in the world, just fix it.

"Let's talk quickly about taglines, before I share with you the final secret of brand positioning."

Chapter 7 Summary

Simplicity is the key to a great logo. Simplicity's purpose is memorability. Customers can reconstruct a simple logo easily in their mind, making a clearer, more powerful mental image. The stronger the mental image, the more likely they are to remember and choose you.

The four main attributes of famous logos are: simple in a symbolic way, memorable, differentiated from the competition, and tell a story.

The story the logo tells should be closely related to the Sales Moment.

The main benefit of repositioning a brand all at once is you can create synergy between the Sales Moment you want to own and the name, logo, tagline, and campaignable image—creating a vastly more powerful brand.

Key Questions

1. Is your logo easy for the customer to recreate in their mind?

2. Does your logo tell a story that communicates your Sales Moment?

Chapter 8

CREATING TAGLINES WITH SPARK

"Taglines are my favorite branding element. I'm stunned by the number of companies that don't have taglines," I said. "It's clearly a best practice in marketing, so you can only conclude, people don't understand their purpose or how to create taglines.

"There seems to be two common mistakes with taglines. The first, you fell into..."

"That would be not having one," Peter said. "We just couldn't think of anything I liked."

I shot him a look and raised an eyebrow. "Oh yeah," he said, "we couldn't think of anything strategic."

"The second mistake is making the tagline a business description of their goods and services. This approach doesn't differentiate a company from other competitors who supply similar product. It would be like Nike saying, *athletic apparel company for active people* instead of *Just do it.* Or De Beers saying, *the world's largest diamond supplier* instead of *A Diamond is Forever.*

"Great taglines bring the brand to life by communicating why it's relevant to the target customer. They call up the Sales Moment. It's your first ad headline and one of your best opportunities to own an idea. You're showing the soul of your company. Every company needs a tagline or you're missing an opportunity to shout why you're relevant to your customer. This is true for B-to-B, B-to-C, or even Business to Government.

"Taglines that build a brand and drive sales can be divided into three types." I wrote on the board PROMISE, CALL TO ACTION, MEMORY. "Promise taglines are based on a key brand attribute. Call to Action taglines invite customers to join because they share the company's philosophy. Memory taglines use a poetic device playing off the name or logo to help people remember the brand.

"Let's think of some great taglines. Consider Timex, *It takes a licking and keeps on ticking*. Which type is that?"

"That's a promise, based on Timex trying to own sturdy reliable watches."

"That was created in 1956 and you still know it. Pretty amazing, isn't it. How valuable was that tagline to selling watches?

"Consider Apple, *Think Different.*"

"That's a Call to Action tagline," Peter said looking at the list. "It's kind of an in-your-face play on IBM's *Think* philosophy, isn't it? As you said, it invites you to join because you share Apple's philosophy."

"Good. How about, *Be all you can be?*"

"That's a great Call to Action tagline," Peter said.

"It also rhymes with Army, but it's mostly a Call to Action tagline," I said. "How about *Maybe she's born with it. Maybe it's Maybelline?*"

Peter thought for a second. "That's what you were calling a Memory tagline. The maybe three times, helps you recall Maybelline."

"One of the interesting techniques is you can do Memory taglines with the company name, even the logo, or even off what the product looks like. Prudential's logo is the Rock of Gilbrator and until the mid-80's they used the slogan, *Own a Piece of the Rock.*

"If I say, *You can't top the copper top*, you say..."

"That's Duracell, because their batteries look so distinctive. That's good product design," Peter said.

"And good marketing to call out that distinctive feature from other batteries. It's also a little bit of a brand promise, isn't it? That their battery lasts longer, can't be topped. So you see how you can mix and match techniques to create a memorable tagline that helps you own the Sales Moment.

"The important thing is not to get caught up in whether it's a Promise tagline or a Call to Action tagline. Sometimes it's both. Or a type that leans toward another type. The point is to use these techniques as a starting point. This helps you discover very powerful, very specific creative that is relevant to your target customer."

"Can you give me an example from something you've done?"

"Sure. We recently created the tagline for an asset

management company, *TransparentValue*. They are the only company in the world that can tell you in a mouse-click how many stores Starbucks has to open to justify its current stock price or how many listings eBay needs to justify their stock price. They can do it for over 2,000 stocks. It is revolutionary stuff."

"How do they do that?"

"The founders Julian Koski and Armen Arus are brilliant. They built an enormous real-time fundamental database of large cap stocks and they are also building out emerging markets around the world. The database works backwards from the current stock price to imply the Required Business Performance for each company. Looking at 10 years of past company performance, the TransparentValue database assigns a probability of company management achieving the performance necessary to support the current stock price. Then, they bet on the companies with the highest likelihood of success. It's Warren Buffet in a box."

"Can you give me an example of how they work?" Peter asked.

"Sure. Let's say TransparentValue determines that Home Depot has to open 79 stores to justify a $37 stock price. And by looking at their audited financials, knows that in the last twelve months Home Depot opened 119 stores. What is the probability then that Home Depot can do better than opening 79 stores in the next twelve months?"

"Pretty good I would imagine," Peter said. "They've already shown they can do it."

"Then what would happen?"

"The stock would likely increase."

"So TransparentValue knows it's a good stock to pick, and in a blink, gets in while the old-fashioned hedge fund analysts are still going over their spread sheets, talking about it, and maybe missing the opportunity before the stock runs.

"TransparentValue recently completed a major partnership deal with Dow Jones in 2008 to create a family of indexes based on their RBP methodology. One of the things TransparentValue demonstrated was a seven-year backtest of the Dow Jones Industrial Average from May of 2000 to May 2007. It showed the Dow Jones Industrial Average achieved a cumulative return of 28.45% versus 72.19% weighting the same stocks using the TransparentValue RBP method. Same stocks, same risk, just a smarter weighting in the index. TransparentValue has a much better approach."

"What's their tagline?"

"*TransparentValue. See the market clearly*™."

"That's good. I see what you mean. It's a Promise, a Call to Action, and a Memorability tagline. *Clearly* plays off the name, right?"

"True. It's all three types. TransparentValue's tagline screams their Sales Moment. So you see, the tagline process is the same as for naming. Coming from the Sales Moment, you create taglines using all three methods and sometimes overlapping. You identify which types and lines help you best own the Sales Moment and which is most memorable. Then you search the trademark database to make sure it's available for federal registration."

Peter nodded in general agreement.

"Other guidelines to consider is shorter is generally better. Though this is not necessarily the case. You want to say something strong. Ameriquest's *The Official Sponsor of the American Dream* is long, but a great Call to Action line."

"Give me one more famous example," Peter requested.

"Consider Volvo, *For Life*. What are Volvo cars known for?"

"Safety. Keeping your family safe, if there was ever a collision."

"You see how those two simple words sum up the Sales Moment that tilts sales in Volvo's favor for a particular type of customer. As long as families are interested in safety, that brand position will work. It's Volvo's positioning; their promise; their philosophy. But it's more. That tagline also provides direction for what kind of cars Volvo needs to design and build year after year. So later, we'll talk about how branding not only increases sales through focus, it also increases efficiency internally by signaling to people every day what they should be working on."

"James, you believe that branding can fix a lot of ills in business, don't you?"

"It's not about believing. I've seen it. If you use these techniques for your company, you'll see it too, both internally and externally.

"Now I want to tell you about one of the most powerful techniques in Brand Marketing. How to create an advertising campaign that both builds brand and creates sales."

Chapter 8 Summary

Every company needs a tagline. Taglines are a great opportunity to shout why a company is relevant to target customers. Taglines are the soul of a company.

The two most common mistakes with taglines are not having one or using a generic description of the company's goods and services, which does not differentiate the company from competition who supply the same product.

Great taglines come in three types:

1. Promise taglines that are based on a key brand attribute.

2. Call to Action taglines that invite customers to join because they share the company's philosophy.

3. Memory taglines that use a poetic device playing off the name or logo to help people remember your brand.

Key Questions

1. Does your company tagline quickly explain why the brand is relevant to your target customer, and differentiate you from the competition?

Chapter 9

THE FOUR TYPES OF ADVERTISING CAMPAIGNS THAT BUILD BRAND AND DRIVE SALES

"In the history of the world, there have been only four types of advertising campaigns that both build brands and drive sales." As I spoke, I wrote on the white board: 1) THE WORD HOOK, 2) THE CHARACTER HOOK, 3) THE REPEATABLE THEME, 4) THE CONSISTENT LAYOUT. Peter wrote them in his note pad as well, waiting for further explanation.

"Without exception, the most popular and most successful advertising campaigns have used one or more of these techniques, making them well-tested best practices in creating ad campaigns. So why is this so important to you?"

"According to your logic," Peter answered. "If my company is not using best practices we're less likely to succeed," Peter said.

"Exactly. That's how I knew when we first sat down, that your marketing never made money for you or your company.

I looked at your website, your ads, and your brochures. I didn't see one of these campaign types. Instantly, I knew that your marketing wasn't working."

"Is that what it was? Why are you so certain these campaign types make a such a difference?" Peter asked.

"Let me explain how each campaign type works. Then, I want you to ask me that again. It's an important question."

I pointed to THE WORD HOOK on the board. "The Word Hook is a repeatable catch phrase from ad to ad. A good example of the Word Hook is Verizon's *Can you hear me now?* Or Mastercard's *Priceless* campaign. You know... *an evening out with friends... having the best story...*"

"*Priceless.*" Peter said. "Sure everyone knows that."

"Who's your cell phone carrier?" I asked.

"Verizon," Peter responded.

"How come?"

"I didn't really think about. I guess, I didn't want to have any dropped calls. I wanted to be able to call from anywhere."

"You just described the Sales Moment, didn't you?"

"Yeah. I guess I did." A flash of excitement came over his face. "That's what their ads were too. When they started, they had that kid in a dark blue jacket walking all over testing his phone, saying, *Can you hear me now?* Hell, I say that when I'm on the cell. Verizon knew exactly what I wanted."

"That's why it worked. Verizon boiled the Sales Moment down to that one Word Hook we all say and became the nation's number one wireless carrier."

"That's good." Peter said, still visibly excited. "Very smart."

"Another classic Word Hook would be the Absolut Campaign. For example, *Absolut Manhattan* featuring an arial view of Central Park in the shape of a bottle. *Absolut Golden Gate* featuring the archway of the Golden Gate Bridge in the same distinctive shape."

"Sure. Those ads are brilliant."

"Consider this Peter. Since 1980, when that campaign was conceived, over 1,500 Absolut ads have used that Word Hook. In 1999, Absolut commanded an amazing 58% market share for vodka—an alcohol that is defined as colorless, tasteless, and odorless. Wouldn't you like to command 58% of the market?"

"Who wouldn't?"

"The Word Hook is like the chorus of a good pop song. They're catchy. Maybe, even insidious. Everybody knows how to play along. Eventually, it becomes so well known, achieves such marketing greatness, it can even serve as a joke."

"Like the *What's up guys.*"

"Sure. Think even further back to 1984. In the middle of a televised debate, Walter Mondale totally disses Gary Hart by saying "When I hear your new ideas I'm reminded of that ad, *Where's the beef?* The audience roared.

"But here's the real punch line. Over twenty years later, you're more likely to remember Wendy's *Where's the beef?* than Gary Hart or Walter Mondale."

"True. Very true." Peter smiled.

"Our Account Director, Todd Brenard, was the Account Strategist on *Where's the Beef?* and the *Russian Fashion Show* campaign for Wendy's when Saatchi & Saatchi did that break-through work."

"Really?"

"Sure, we have a whole team of people who learned best practices on major national brands and now prefer working with the owners of midsized businesses. You get to look the people in the eye, whose life your making a difference in. It's much more rewarding."

I pointed to the second campaign type, the Character Hook. "The Character Hook uses a hero, villain, or victim to embody a key attribute of the brand. Think of Ronald McDonald. He's a hero of happiness. He was created in 1963 to help McDonald's own family fast food." I emphasized the word *family*.

"How effective was this character? Consider that 96% of school children in the United States can identify Ronald McDonald. Only Santa Claus is more commonly recognized. McDonald's didn't set out to own fast food. They wanted to own *family* fast food. So let me ask you, are families with kids more likely to go to McDonald's, Burger King or Wendy's?"

"McDonald's," Peter answered instantly.

"Ronald helped them do that. And that strong positioning of happiness led naturally to the Happy Meal which secured their audience."

"What's an example of a Character Hook villian?" Peter asked.

"How about Joe Isuzu, the sneaky car salesman. The savvy, intelligent customers Isuzu was targeting, found Joe Isuzu appealing."

"Those commercials were hysterical," Peter said.

"Peter, you can still remember those commercials from 1985. That's how strong the character was."

Peter was cracking the campaign types wide open. I decided to keep challenging him. "Can you name a victim that's a Character Hook?"

He thought for a few minutes. "I've got it. The Maytag Repairman. He's a victim of great product dependability. He just sits waiting for the phone to ring because the washing machine is so good, it doesn't break down."

"The Maytag Repairman is a perfect example. That character was created in 1967. He kept Maytag top of mind, which helped build the company into a juggernaut. The company and character were sold to Maytag's rival, the Whirlpool Corporation, in 2006 for a remarkable $1.6 billion."

"So the Geico Gecko or AFLAC duck would be character hooks as well?" Peter offered.

"Perfect examples," I exclaimed. I made a mental note to use those in future presentations. "Those characters help you remember the brand. Having potential customers remember your brand is half the battle. What they know about the brand is the other half."

Peter nodded really getting into this conversation.

"Characters are tremendous for breaking through advertising clutter and establishing emotional connections with customers. They are vivid, intriguing, and cause us to care about them. If you care about a character, then you care about the brand. Ever wonder, what Snoopy has to do with life insurance?"

"That one is strange to me. What does Snoopy have to do

with MetLife?"

"Emotional transference. Buying life insurance is something people would rather not think about. Few people enjoy facing the fact that they could die at any time. So buying life insurance is not a feel good experience. However, people like Snoopy. By using Snoopy, people like MetLife. Snoopy makes the company more approachable than other insurers."

"Isn't that kind of silly for a business as serious as insurance?" Peter said raising a common concern.

"Just look at how well it worked. Today, MetLife is the largest U.S. life insurer. Any insurance company could have licensed Snoopy if they had identified the Sales Moment for life insurance. MetLife is also the number-one provider of property and casualty insurance in the workplace. Meaning, the Character Hook worked for both their business-to-consumer and business-to-business side. People remembered the Snoopy company and felt good buying from them.

I pointed to the third type of successful advertising campaign: the Repeatable Theme. The Repeatable Theme is a situation that plays out again and again calling out the need for a company's product.

"Examples of a repeatable theme include the York Peppermint Patty ads created by Cliff Freeman. Or the Citibank anti-money, *Live Richly* campaign. You give me an example of a repeatable theme?"

Peter thought for a moment and said, "Those strange Mentos, *Freshmaker* ads."

"What do you like about those ads?"

"I'm not sure. Maybe it's because you already know the punch line. It's satisfying to be in on the joke, before it comes. It's the same joke played out in different situations."

"That's it. I agree. Repeatable themes make the target customer feel like they have the inside track. They know how to play along and thus feel connected to your brand.

"The final type is the Consistent Layout. The Consistent Layout uses a unique, design look then repeats those elements at each touchpoint. This allows customers to easily identify your company in a blink. The more distinct these elements are from your competitors, the easier it is to stand out from the clutter.

"You have to fly all the time for your business. Can you describe the Continental ads?"

Peter leaned back in his chair like he was settling in for a long flight. "Sure, it's the blue globe, yellow trim around the outside. With a white all cap headline at the top."

"So how do they use it?" I asked.

"They put that design on everything from the ticket envelopes, to bag tags, to cocktail napkins. It's on the carpeting in their terminal. And, of course, on their ads. Though I would have thought you wouldn't like the globe image."

"Mostly, I admire Continental's consistency. They embraced that institutional look completely, went with it and it worked. That Consistent Layout has helped Continental become one of the largest, most profitable airlines in the world. You can easily recreate the brand image in your mind. And to be fair, a globe is a little more on the Sales Moment for people who want to travel the continents. It also helps you remember their name.

Doesn't it?"

"Give me another example," Peter knocked the ball into my court.

"Consider Apple's iPod ads. That's a Consistent Layout. Can you describe them?"

"Sure," he said leaning forward. "They have these cool silhouetted people on bright backgrounds. I think they're dancing or something like that. You can see the iPod clearly."

"Do they look like anyone else's ad?"

"No, they are pretty different." We both smiled at the pun he had just made on Apple's tagline.

"And that's one of the keys to the Consistent Layout, isn't it? You want to zig where everyone else is zagging. If everyone else is corporate blue, you want to be another color. If everyone else is playful design, you want to go serious. Consistent design is about consciously standing out from the crowd and keeping your proprietary brand design going on everything.

"But more importantly," I continued taking a seat at the table, "the Consistent Layout serves a deeper purpose. Consistency instills trust. When a company plants its flag around one design look and feel, customers feel comfortable with that brand faster and longer. In an uncertain world, the consumer's deep desire for something they can consistently count on is soothed by the Consistent Layout."

Peter nodded. He could see how the campaigns worked. It was time for his question. "So the point I asked you about earlier," he began. "Why do you think using one of these techniques is so critical for a business like mine?"

"Context," I answered. "Think about what you are up against. Most advertising in midsized businesses is created without really understanding the marketing environment. Let's think about it together."

"Another thought experiment?"

"When a target customer sees your website, print ad, TV ad, brochure, direct mail piece, or hears your radio spot," I counted customer touchpoints off with my fingers, "it may be the first time that person is encountering your brand."

"Fair enough," Peter commented.

"Now the average American encounters between 300-3,000 advertising impressions per day, depending on which study you believe and how you define an impression. The numbers are growing in every country. People are simply bombarded by too much information every day. You're overwhelmed by it. For example, when we get done with this meeting, you're going to be scared to look at your email."

"It's true. Too many messages every day. Too much news. Too many ads."

"So visualize what you will do? It will be the same thing your target customers do. You'll scan a marketing piece in a blink, looking for a handle to process the information. Without a handle, you are likely to reject it simply by moving on to something else."

Peter repeated the key phrase. "So my business needs a handle."

"Here's the thing. In the current marketing environment,

you're not just competing against brands in your industry for market share. You're competing against everything in existence for mind share. Your greatest adversary is *ignorance*. Your target customer simply isn't thinking about your company. They can't remember your company or what it stands for."

"That's tough," Peter said.

"You need to use one of these campaign types to change that. And these campaign types work for two key reasons. The first is these campaign types function as handles—entering points that allow information to be processed quickly to explain your relevance to a potential customer. Watch closely how this works," I said touching different places on the table's surface as I went. "Because information can be processed quickly, a sales proposition can be made. If the proposition is compelling and matches their Sales Moment, a sale can be driven. All this starts with a campaign handle." I concluded pointing back to the four campaign types on the white board.

"The second reason these campaign types are essential is they create powerful mental images. Again, mental images are the link between branding and sales. We talked at length earlier about how the mind thinks in pictures and how little movies of unmet needs trigger the sale. You remember, don't you?"

"Sure. I found that Sales Moment discussion really interesting."

"So now you have a complete understanding of what you have to do in Step One: Positioning a Brand through the Sales Moment. The company name, logo, tagline, and campaignable image all come together to convey a single mental image that tilts sales in your favor. And, of course, it's all based on the Sales Moment."

"If I do this, how will I know when to change the ad campaign?"

"That's just it. If you positioned the brand correctly in Step One and are following best practices for creating all the brand elements, you won't have to change the advertising campaign. Because, it will be working."

"But when do you change it?" Peter asked again.

"Change your advertising campaign only when the current one isn't growing sales. It's pretty simple really. If your advertising isn't working, change it. If your sales are no longer growing, re-evaluate the brand before creating the next advertising campaign to avoid making more expensive advertising mistakes.

"Don't keep throwing things against the wall, like you have been, waiting for something to stick. Be strategic. Advertising campaigns most often fail simply because the ownable Sales Moment wasn't correctly identified. You understand that now. Then, they fail because one of the four campaign techniques that we just talked about weren't used."

"Well, we certainly didn't do it the way you're recommending. And you can be damn sure we won't keep doing it wrong," Peter said adamantly.

I nodded sensing the depth of his commitment to change.

"If you ever find yourself using one of these techniques and you're still not experiencing great results, then you haven't correctly identified your Sales Moment. And of course, quality of design execution is always an important factor. It's vital to be the visual leader in your category."

"What does that mean," Peter asked.

"The best looking through great design.

"Another reason sales stop growing is because the ownable Sales Moment has shifted due to changes in the marketplace. When necessity dictates, companies must change their message.

"The key is to let sales be the sole indicator if a campaign is working or not. This means don't change your advertising campaign because you are bored. One of the saddest things I've seen in marketing is to watch successful companies change their ad campaigns because they are bored, or someone else comes on board and they want to put their mark on a brand, or they think their customers want something new. Let sales determine this. The James Group only changes things that aren't working. Otherwise, leave it alone.

"Absolut wisely ran their campaign 26 years before changing it, when their market share started to decline in 2005 due to designer vodkas with additives coming into the market. Nike has run variations of the *Just Do It* campaigns since 1982. Continental has been running the blue globe ads for over a decade. That takes brand discipline, because they are all probably very bored. Laugh all the way to the bank and find another hobby other than your marketing for entertainment. Marketing is to make money. Not to entertain you.

"It is also interesting to note, from 1987 to 1997, MasterCard tried five advertising campaigns—and failed to narrow the gap with Visa. When McCann created the *Priceless* campaign another spot actually tested better. But they knew they had correctly identified the Sales Moment in *Priceless* and that they were using best practices in advertising with the Word Hook. The rest is history.

"Bottom line. To build brand and drive sales you need to position the brand through the ownable Sales Moment; reflect the Sales Moment in the company name, logo, and tagline; and use one of the four types of advertising campaigns to drive it home. This process will provide the highest probability of marketing success."

Peter nodded. We had summed up the first step of *The Perfection of Marketing* process succinctly, but there was something visibly bothering Peter.

"What is it, Peter?"

Peter sighed again. "I just feel like our Director of Marketing, Jason Matthews, should have told me all this."

I took a slow breath before responding to gather my thoughts. "I suspect he tried. Peter, you're a tough guy to give bad news. If you're honest, you probably didn't want to hear about your brand's weaknesses. It's usually easier and safer to have an outside consultant deliver the hard news. I have a feeling that has something to do with why I am here today. We help a lot of Marketing Directors that way.

"The other thing is back to our brand designer/graphic designer discussion. Developing a brand is usually a different discipline than managing one. In my experience, most Marketing Directors are better trained in how to select and manage the implementation of marketing tactics. They excel at the discipline which comes in Step Two and Step Three. Most Marketing Directors have very little experience creating brands from scratch. In large advertising agencies, where Marketing Directors often come from, they're usually managing an established, well-defined brand. Unless you've hired a marketing person who has created dozens of brands from scratch, in my opinion, it makes more sense to work with someone whose specialty is positioning brands, who knows the Step One branding techniques inside and out."

Peter nodded again. I felt his discomfort dissolve. He was ready to move forward. "I like what I heard in Step One. Once we have defined our Sales Moment and what the brand should look like and talk like, then what do we do?"

"You move on to Step Two: Rolling Out the Brand Consistently. Do you want me to continue?"

Chapter 9 Summary

In the history of the world, there only have been four types of advertising campaigns that both build brands and drive sales. They are: the Word Hook, the Character Hook, the Repeatable Theme, the Consistent Layout.

1. The Word Hook is a repeatable catch phrase from ad to ad.

2. The Character Hook uses a hero, villain, or victim to embody a key attribute of the brand.

3. The Repeatable Theme is a situation that plays out again and again calling out the need for a company's product.

4. The Consistent Layout uses a unique design look then repeats those elements at each touchpoint.

The average American encounters between 300-3,000 advertising impressions per day, and the numbers are increasing for every country. Your greatest adversary is ignorance—that your potential customer is not thinking about your company.

These campaign types serve as handles—entering points that allow information to be processed quickly to explain your relevance to a potential customer. These campaign types also create powerful mental images allowing the potential customer to remember your brand.

If you are not using one or more of these techniques, there is the highest probability that your marketing is not making money for you.

You need to change your advertising campaign only when the current one isn't growing sales. When a company correctly identifies it's Sales Moment and uses these techniques, they can run the same advertising campaign for many years.

Key Questions

1. Is your company using one of these four types of advertising campaigns?

2. Are you using your campaign image in each of your marketing touchpoints (web, brochures, direct mail, tradeshows, PR, etc.)?

3. Is your advertising campaign growing sales for your company?

For visual examples of the brand positioning work through the Sales Moment visit www.PerfectionofMarketing.com. For assistance developing your company's brand, contact The James Group at 212-243-2022 or visit www.thejamesgroup.com.

Step II:
Rolling Out the Brand
Consistently

Chapter 10

STEP II: ROLLING OUT THE BRAND CONSISTENTLY

"O.K. James, I'll make you a deal again," said Peter.
If I like what I hear in Step Two, I'll let you tell me about Step Three."

"Fair enough. But before I explain how to roll out the brand consistently, I have an idea."

"What's that?"

"I noticed a really tall man in a purple dress shirt earlier. Actually, he's walked by the conference room a number of times, looking very interested in what we are doing in here. I suspect that's your Director of Marketing."

"Yes. That would be Jason. I wanted the two of us to meet to give you the freedom to speak freely."

"I understand. What the company's brand stands for and looks like is the responsibility of the CEO. Without question, you have to be involved with all brand decisions. If it's all right with you, I would like to have your Director of Marketing join in on this discussion. If we're going to work together in the future, we'll be working primarily with your Director of

Marketing to roll out and maintain the brand. So, it's best to create consensus from the beginning about what should be done."

"Makes sense," Peter responded. "I'll bring Jason in. You can bring him up to speed on our conversation. It will give me a chance to check my emails and make a few calls."

Jason towered over me in size. He had the distinguished look of a seasoned executive with the easy charm of an accomplished sales manager. He made polite conversation inquiring into how long The James Group had been around, the size of our shop, who our biggest clients were, and what industries we had prior experience in. But as soon as Peter excused himself from the conference room, he asked his real question: "What brings you in today?"

How I wish I could tell each Director of Marketing they have nothing to fear from The James Group. We aren't after their jobs. Far from it: there has to be someone in each company who is the day-to-day brand enforcer—keeping the company on brand with all its business decisions. In the absence of a formal Director of Marketing, either it's the CEO's job to evangelize the brand, or they empower someone with that additional responsibility. Many times, both CEO and the Director of Marketing serve the purpose. Every company needs an internal brand ambassador to make the brand real each day. What percentage of our clients have had Marketing Directors? I honestly couldn't say. *The Perfection of Marketing* worked perfectly in either case. It was always a collaborative process, leveraging the internal expertise within a company, joining it with our own. Our mutual success couldn't have come otherwise, without agency and client working closely together.

"I'm here as a potential resource for you to help with your brand," I responded. "Peter brought me in. I wanted us all to speak together as you two ultimately make the decision about what should be done with your brand."

Jason relaxed a bit and we had a quick conversation about the process Peter and I had discussed in Step One. Though fluent with the marketing techniques we were recommending, Jason conceded that he had been unable to convince Peter to address serious weaknesses in the company's brand. Jason felt hampered by a limited marketing budget and the lack of strategic creative support. He was trying to do the best he could within the parameters he had been given permission to operate.

"Jason, I think you'll find The James Group to be a good ally for you. Our process gets the CEO more involved in the brand positioning process. We find it's essential this key person understands deeply why certain tough choices must be made. Then, you both can look at the fully developed brand campaign, understand the strategy completely, and make a business decision. It will be the simplest of tests. If you believe it will help your company make more money, you move forward with the brand recommendation from Step One. If not, you kill it."

"Does that happen often?" Jason asked. "That the Marketing Director and CEO don't accept the brand recommendation?"

"Rarely. *The Perfection of Marketing* process has been carefully fine-tuned to involve everyone in creating the brand.

The purpose is to create consensus. In twelve years, we have had only three brand recommendations killed."

"How did you feel about that?" Jason asked.

"Good that it almost never happens. But it's a very sad thing when it does. It hurts to miss an opportunity to help someone. Even then, the companies later went back and implemented the strategy, but not the creative. So at least, there is some acknowledgement that we gave them the very best recommendation possible."

"It's hard to get people to change," Jason said.

"True," I responded. "But much easier once you clearly define the Sales Moment. Everything flows from that." I knew what he was hinting: getting Peter Gibbons to change his brand and marketing approach was a tough battle. I understood Jason's pain. Marketing is notoriously misunderstood and under-budgeted in midsized businesses—Marketing Directors sent to conquer kingdoms with slingshots in a sky missile world. As there is so little room for error, the potent pain relief The James Group offers is best practices.

"This is why we concentrate on branding fundamentals with the owners and chiefs of companies," I continued. "We find that once a CEO understands the brand marketing process and sees what their brand will look like in the market place, they are far more confident investing behind it. You and I know what needs to be done. I'm sure we can do it with the right strategy, right creative, and proper resources."

Peter Gibbons returned to the conference room. "Interesting discussion, isn't it?"

"All good things," Jason said. "We've talked about a lot of this before, but it's always good to be reminded."

"I told James if we like what we hear in Step Two, we would listen more to his Step Three. If not, he gets the boot."

"Thank you, Peter," I began. "It's good to have you both here. What the brand stands for is primarily the responsibility of the CEO. How to roll it out and communicate it consistently is primarily the responsibility of the Marketing Director. We've already talked about how to build the brand foundation in Step One. That was the hard part—figuring out what your Sales Moment is. By doing that first, the probability of success with your marketing tactics dramatically increases. Once you position the brand through the Sales Moment, promoting that moment is comparatively easy. Much of what I have to say about Step Two, Rolling Out a Brand Consistently, will be old hat to Jason. But I'll share with you a few of our special techniques to keep it interesting for Jason in particular."

Jason nodded as I went to the white board. I felt each of us in the room had the basis for a good collaborative conversation about rolling out a brand.

In blue pen, I wrote Step Two: CONSISTENT ROLLOUT. I drew nine medium-sized circles, as if moving around the face of a clock, and then connected them with arced lines to make a larger circle. It looked like an old-fashioned rotary phone dial. In the center I wrote: BRAND.

"Being an expert is more than knowing what has to be done; it's knowing the order in which things should be done. In Step One, you defined your Sales Moment and how to convey it. The purpose of Step Two is to communicate your Sales Moment consistently to your target customer—to turn every customer touchpoint into a branding and sales opportunity. Again, in Step One, figure out what your Sales Moment is. And in Step Two, promote your Sales Moment. To do this, every marketing tactic must come out of the brand Sales Moment. There should never be confusion or inconsistency as to what is being said and what it should look like." I pointed to the word BRAND in the center of Step Two.

"We'll talk about several of the key tactics in detail. But let's first get an overview of how to roll out the brand." I wrote PEOPLE in the second circle on the brand rollout dial, deliberately leaving the first circle empty. It was PLANNING, but I would come back to it. They wanted to focus on tactics. "Before you spend one dime on advertising. The place to start is with your people. You have to get everyone in management and everyone who works in the company on the same page. This first tactic, training your people in the brand, will make the brand real."

I wrote WEBSITE in the third circle of the brand rollout dial. "While you are training your people you redesign your website focusing on three main points. Does it communicate your Sales Moment using your campaignable image? Is it sticky, meaning people will want to spend time there? And, is it optimized for search engines so you can score high in organic search rankings?"

"I'm interested to hear about techniques for search engines," Jason said.

"Good. We have some definite best practices for search engines, which I will explain in detail later."

"As you create the website, you design the brochure." I wrote BROCHURES in the fourth circle and then PARTNERS in the fifth circle. "Partners are people who have access to your target customer, particularly those who don't compete with you."

"Jason," I said pointing at the first group of tactics, PEOPLE, WEBSITE, BROCHURES, PARTNERS. "What is the pattern with these first tactics?"

Jason thought for a moment. "You are moving from the inside out, concentrating first on the tactics that cost the least."

"Precisely," I responded.

"That will give us the most bang for our buck," Peter said joining in.

"Focus on these foundation tactics first, because you're already doing them," I said. "It doesn't cost you much more to do them right. Does it?"

"What do you mean?" Peter asked.

"You're already paying heavy salaries," I stated.

"That's for certain," Peter quipped.

"Particularly for your sales force. It doesn't cost that much to retrain them to focus on the Sales Moment that tilts sales in your favor. That training will create more sales."

Peter and Jason nodded in unison.

"You are already hosting a website. People are going to your website. It needs to be on message as well."

"Well, not enough people are going to our website," Jason

reminded us.

"Not to worry; we'll fix that when we talk about Search Engine Optimization. In the same way, you're already printing brochures," I added. "You may as well print the single message that tilts sales in your favor."

I pointed to the PARTNER circle. "You already have vendors and no doubt some partners you work with. What do they really know about you? What do they say to refer someone to you?"

The room got very quiet as Peter looked at Jason and Jason looked at Peter.

"I don't think any of our vendors have ever referred a customer to us," Peter said.

"I don't think so either," Jason added.

"O.K., we need to talk about Partner strategies in some detail." I said making a mental note to devote more time for them to Partner strategies. "So you see," I continued, pointing at the brand rollout dial, "The first four tactics are all stuff that you are already spending time and money on. You could make them more effective by using your campaignable image to communicate your Sales Moment."

"What are the next things in brand rollout?" Peter asked.

"PR, ads, followed by direct mail, and event marketing." I wrote each tactic in the remaining empty circles. "Ads include print, Internet banners or paid search, TV, and radio."

"You're saying we should do TV?" asked Jason.

"It's best not to rule out any tactics until we evaluate the value of your customer. You might do extremely well with a local cable buy for $200-300 a 30-second spot on a news channel like CNBC. Or, other tactics may make more sense. I'm trying to give you an idea of the order in which things would go."

"Why did you put event marketing last?" Peter asked.

"This is a general order to roll out the brand," I said gesturing toward the brand rollout dial. "You're moving from the least expensive tactics to the most expensive. The order of the first four is pretty fixed. You don't want to approach partners until your people are well-trained, your website that partners will look at is on message, and the brochure you will leave them communicates your Sales Moment.

"The last four then are more flexible. You can do them in the order that makes most sense for your situation. We like trade shows, but generally they provide lower ROI in isolation, so we prefer to do them with support from the other tactics to increase their effectiveness."

Peter looked slightly confused and I hadn't addressed his question straight on.

"Let me back in to your question. The reason we generally do PR first is even a brand change creates buzz and good announcements. Also sending press releases through online distribution companies increases backlinks which increase search engine rankings. Direct mail can be a great tactic, but even better when people have heard of your company, which is why we tend to do some measure of advertising first. We prefer print and TV first to radio as they are better at creating mental images that are key to brands. We're a very visual culture. Radio is a good reminder medium once the target customer has a mental image of your brand. We can also use direct mail and trade ads to invite key target customers to visit you at an important trade show in the industry. This is why we tend to put event marketing last."

"I'm assuming the degree you rely on each tactic varies dramatically from customer to customer," Jason said.

"To be certain," I said. "For the last four tactics, B-to-B customers behave much differently than B-to-C customers. But they are the same in one regard—all these tactics must come out of the Sales Moment of the brand.

"We'll talk specifically about how we choose tactics and the marketing mix when we get to Step Three, but for now lets circle back and talk about that first tactic. Training your people in the brand to make it real."

Chapter 10 Summary

In Step One, you defined your Sales Moment, what the brand will look like and talk like. In Step Two, you communicate your Sales Moment consistently to your target customer—turning every customer touchpoint into a branding and sales opportunity.

Every marketing tactic comes out of the brand Sales Moment. There should never be confusion or inconsistency as to what is being said and what the brand looks like.

Brands should be communicated from the inside out, concentrating first on the foundation tactics that cost the least: Planning, People, Website, Brochures, and Partners. The order of the first foundation tactics is pretty fixed. Then come more external marketing activities of PR, ads (print, Internet, TV, radio), direct mail, and event marketing. The order of the external tactics are more flexible.

B-to-B customers behave much differently than B-to-C customers for the last set of external tactics. But they are the same in one regard—all these tactics come out of the Sales Moment of the brand.

Key Questions

1. Do your marketing tactics (what your people say, website, brochures, marketing to partners, PR, ads, direct mail, and event marketing) come out of the brand Sales Moment?

2. Do all your marketing tactics consistently convey what the brand looks like and talks like?

3. Are you making the most of your lowest cost foundational tactics of People, Website, Brochures, and Partners?

Chapter 11

GET YOUR PEOPLE ON BRAND FIRST

"The most efficient companies eliminate ambiguity," I began. "Not to stifle thinking, but as a result of thinking long and hard about the best ways to do things to create consistent results."

"The brand then is a management tool for what to give up and what to take up, what to say and not say, what to do and not do." *Eliminating ambiguity is the key to all wisdom,* I thought to myself. "Tactically, a brand is all about consistency." I turned to the white board and pointed to PEOPLE in the circle at one o'clock on the brand rollout dial, then returned to my place at the table.

A platoon of soldiers running in cadence, the sound of their boots striking a tree-lined street came to my mind—such power moving in unison as if one being. "For me, the best thing about growing up on Army bases around the world was it gave me incredible insight into the power of training. I particularly remember the six years of my life I spent in Fort Benning, Georgia as a boy. It's an enormous Army Post.

"At any given time, there are over 100,000 soldiers going through Basic Infantry Training or Airborne Ranger School, as well as officers going through Basic Combat Training and Advanced Individual Training.

"If the hardest thing in the world is to get people to put aside their individual self-cherishing needs and work as a team, the most unnatural thing has to be to get people to run toward bullets. Through training, the Army has found a way to accomplish both. Now one could debate the value of these endeavors, but truly amazing is the effectiveness of the Army's training. The essence of the Army's method is clarity and repetition. Clarity and repetition," I said again for emphasis. I could see the phrase resonated particularly with Peter.

"From the time I was a little boy, I can remember soldiers telling me, you are either trained or you are not trained. You either know what to do or you don't. These same principles have to be applied to your business, Peter."

"Are you saying, we run every employee through some sort of basic training where we break them down before building them up?" Jason jabbed sarcastically.

"Of course not," I smiled. "I just want to highlight the essence of any effective training methodology. Clarity and repetition," I said a third time.

"So what do you want us to be clear about?" Peter asked.

"Train your team on what the Sales Moment is for your company. Everyone should know your carrot and be focused on it. Train your team on the specific techniques they can use to make the brand real at each moment of customer contact."

"How do you recommend we do that?" Jason asked.

"By first being clear about what each employee has to take up and give up. To do this, The James Group creates an Employee Brand Playbook for each client, by position, outlining for each employee what has changed and what they must do now."

Peter and Jason were intrigued. They wanted to know more. Seeing an actual book would be easier than explaining conceptually, so I reached in my briefcase, a simple shoulder bag, for two Employee Brand Playbooks that I had permission to share. On the table, I opened the rectangular shaped playbooks we created for Juma, a company that guarantees their work for corporate voice, data, and video IP convergence, and Posillico, a construction company specializing in complex projects. I recalled the development of these brands in my mind. They were two very different cases in which the same brand best practices were used to solve two different challenges. For Juma, it was simplifying complex, new technology services so clients would know what they were buying, and for Posillico, it was finding clear brand differentiation in a mature industry competing primarily on price.

Through customer interviews for Juma, we had discovered that nearly every major company knew they had to do something with IP convergence to reduce costs and increase productivity, but they didn't know how. We found an AT&T Network Convergence Survey that concluded that 77% of executives said IP convergence would be implemented in all or most of their business by 2009. Through competitor analysis, we also saw that no company was planting its flag as the specialists in IP convergence. Clients raved about Juma's ability to solve complex IP convergence issues. CTOs even revealed their greatest worry about undertaking such a system integration project: would it work? This was an enormous opportunity—but fear was the chief obstacle to a sale.

The Sales Moment occurred for Juma when a potential client experienced an expert guiding them through the possibilities of IP convergence, then outlined a worry-free plan for implementation including a guarantee that the implementation would work as designed. For Juma the positioning and tagline were simple: *IP Convergence with a Guarantee*™.

Peter and Jason studied the Employee Brand Playbook. Opposite a four-color image created for the advertising was a letter signed by the top management team, explaining the Sales Moment and brand changes. The next pages explained the new logo, tagline, the advertising campaign, the website strategy, and the new IP Convergence Plan. Then, after getting employees excited about the brand with big four-color images of the creative, the book went to the heart of the issue. Here's what Juma employees had to do to make this brand real.

In a succinct two pages, each person in the company could see their role defined by how they interacted with clients; what the key success drivers were that they would be measured on; and what was different now about their job to make this new brand real.

John and Peter stopped on a spread that explained the logic of how all Juma's services came together. IP convergence consulting and system integration lead to managed services and hosted PBX solutions, and finally telecommunications services performed under another brand The James Group developed called Nectar, *the smoothest transition to VoIP™.*

Flipping to the next two-page spread, Jason and Peter saw The Convergence Architect's job explained in detail. And then the Convergence Engineer's. Further ahead even Executive Management's key drivers to success were defined starting with the first key driver: "Fostering a culture of highest integrity by putting the customer's needs first and living up to your guarantee. And the second: "Continuously training others in the company to duplicate your knowledge, and empowering people to eliminate management bottlenecks."

"I wish my business had this," Peter said picking up the book and looking at its pages in detail.

"This is really a beautiful book," said Jason. "It looks like an annual report."

"It's better than an annual report," I said. "This Employee Brand book creates the numbers that make the annual report look good."

"I bet this was difficult to do," Peter said handing the book to Jason.

"You'd be surprised at how easy it is when you look at your business solely through the lens of a customer's brand experience. It becomes very clear, very fast, what you should give up and take up. Mostly, it's a discipline to get management to sit down over a few days and ask: If we were going to do this business better, how would we do it? We keep them focused and boil down the points to the key things actually needed from each employee to make the brand real and create a successful business. In a matter of weeks, you have it all written down, designed, and you can start training people in it. We usually do a large group session, then individual break-out sessions with each position type. Then, you follow-up in six weeks, to hear how they are doing, what they like, and what they feel they need more help with."

"Can you do the training without the book?" Jason asked.

"Sure, you can start planting seeds with people, but in our experience, there is a real power in writing it down and putting it in a single book where each person not only sees their responsibilities, but what others are expected to do as well."

"Sort of a mutual promise to each other," Jason said.

"Exactly. Now think further about the importance of such an approach," I said to help them see the long-term picture. "Having these brand processes built into the Operations creates a recognizably different experience for customers. Having this level of clarity creates incredible efficiencies as the business grows and needs to hire more people."

Jason looked at the Posillico book. I explained further: "Posillico even uses this brochure in recruiting construction people who want to make a commitment to complex construction problem solving. It helps Posillico identify who to hire."

"So long-term," Peter said, "this will make Posillico a

profoundly different, more valuable kind of construction company."

"Now you see it. Imagine if Juma or Posillico wanted to sell their business. The management teams could share their P&L numbers and point to their practices in this Employee Brand Playbook. They could clearly explain this is how their business works and this is why it is different. A buyer would have a better understanding of the kind of business they are buying."

Peter nodded in agreement.

"There are really only two reasons to own and build a business: 1) to get more life on your terms and 2) to sell it. Building the brand, doing this kind of Employee Brand Playbook with training, then measuring behind it, creates the kind of turnkey business you would want to own and others would want to buy.

"Every now and then, we have clients that just want to skip this step. It's, of course, their choice, as it is their business. But I do wish I could convince them otherwise. Those clients tend to lose their brand discipline faster, require significantly more hand-holding or outright arm-wrestling to keep them on mission. And worse—they grow slower because their people execute poorly due to lack of clarity."

"Would you really tell clients they are off mission?" Jason asked.

"If someone was about to put their hand on a hot stove would you try to stop them?"

"Sure."

"Employee Brand Playbooks keep clients from putting their

hands on hot stoves," I said. "I know you want to talk about building websites for search engine placement, so let's look at this second brand tactic in some detail.

Chapter 11 Summary

The most efficient companies eliminate ambiguity. Not to stifle thinking, but as a result of thinking long and hard about the best ways to do things to create consistent results. The brand then is a management tool for what to give up and what to take up; what to say and not say; what to do and not do.

An Employee Brand Playbook makes the brand real by outlining for each employee, by position, what has changed and what they must do now. It focuses the entire company on the Sales Moment and the specific techniques each person can use to make the brand real at each moment of customer contact.

Training people in the brand realizes the promise of brand rollouts. Lack of training does not. The essence of training is clarity and repetition.

Creating an Employee Brand Playbook with training, then measuring behind it, creates the kind of turnkey business you want to own and others would want to buy. It helps you to hire the right kind of people as the company grows. It also creates incredible business efficiencies as people understand how to deliver on the company's brand promise every day.

Key Questions

1. Has your company put its key methods in writing to create consistency and efficiency?

2. Has everyone in your company been trained on how to contribute to deliver on the company's Sales Moment?

Chapter 12

BUILDING WEBSITES FOR SEARCH ENGINE PLACEMENT

"Before you agreed to meet with me Peter, what did you do?" I said.

"I looked at your website," Peter responded. "If I'm considering doing business with anyone, I look at their website."

"Why?"

"To gauge the quality of the business, I guess. See what they are offering. See if they are worth my time." And there it was. Peter had said almost all that was needed about websites.

"Your potential customers are doing the same thing. You said it. So websites and search engine rankings are essential in business today. Both in how customers find you and what they will think of you." I could see Peter was thinking about his own website. Perhaps realizing the reason I had come to see him after viewing his website—there was a problem."

"So what do you recommend should be on a website?" Peter asked.

"You need to accomplish three things with your website. First, give them a handle to quickly understand your company." Jason wrote down HANDLE in a leather-bound notebook he had brought to the meeting. Its pages had no lines allowing ample room for writing and sketching. "The handle is your campaignable image," I continued. "It gets across your Sales Moment very fast, which is the main reason to choose your company, as we said before. The handle gives a potential customer a reason to stay and investigate longer.

"The biggest challenge of the web is that every door is an exit. Too many websites experience bounces. A bounce is when someone lands on your homepage and decides in three to four seconds that there isn't something there for them. Then, they are gone. Often this occurs because there is just too much information and they don't know where to start. They don't have a compelling reason to read yet. The handle is the compelling reason.

"Jason, do you have a wireless connection here in the conference room?" I asked.

"We do."

"Let's look at some examples of websites. I'll take you to websites we've created that are about your company's size and we can see this first principle of websites in action."

Jason left the conference room to get his laptop. While he was away, Peter spoke candidly. "I'm glad you're here today. I liked what you said earlier about training people. We can certainly do better, particularly with our Sales Force. You don't differentiate between Sales and Marketing, do you?"

"No difference," I said. "Your Sales Force is the primary part of People. That is the first tactic of your marketing. It has to be as effective and on message as your website, print ads, or direct mail. I know some like to separate the two. But as you observed, it is the first piece of the same whole. Each part reinforcing each other. So the sales force has to be addressed for consistent brand rollout."

Jason came back and pulled up an Internet browser. I took him to a B-to-B site: www.roundhousegroup.com. Instantly, he saw a large headline, *Suddenly IT is Sexy,* over an orange duo-tone image of four nude window mannequins.

"That's quite surprising," Peter said.

"And look what you are doing, Peter. You are reading to find out why IT is sexy."

Peter's eyes scanned the top paragraph of copy explaining Roundhouse, an IT company that provides Electronic Data Interface services (EDI) to fashion apparel companies to help them grow their brands at retail. He still was reading.

"We didn't lose you to the bounce," I said. "Instead, we gave you an engaging handle and the Repeatable Theme Hook to draw you in. You quickly learned that this is an IT company exclusively for the fashion and apparel business. If you're a fashion or apparel business, we're speaking in a way that makes sense to you, using images of retail." Jason clicked through the website seeing further images of retail: a woman trying on a dress, or two women walking with shopping bags. "Rather than talk tech or look tech, we are showing fashion companies the benefits of using Roundhouse EDI processing to track their merchandise from the warehouse to the retail floor."

"What was the result of this campaign?" Jason asked.

"After 10 years of business, Roundhouse revenues jumped 50% in eight weeks and profit margins doubled. We put ads in Women's Wear Daily, which is the main trade paper. We actually had to pull the ads because it brought in too much business for Roundhouse to operationalize at one time."

"That's a nice problem to have," Peter said.

"The important thing is that the image you saw in the ads is the same as the website. Roundhouse went on to become one of the preferred EDI vendors for JC Penny's and Sears. Meaning, if you wanted to supply goods to either of these major retailers, they recommend you use Roundhouse for EDI logistics."

I then directed them to a B-to-C website: www.teedandbrown.com. "Let me give you another example of how to quickly use the campaign image as a handle to get people into your site." The image was of a lush green lawn that seemed to go on forever. On a blanket a husband and wife sat talking together. The headline asked the question: *What is a Teed and Brown lawn?* The answer in smaller type: *It's where the most important meetings are held.* Then there was the logo, Teed & Brown, which looked like a crest, with the tagline, *Lawn Care for Distinctive Homes.*

"What kind of lawn care company is this?" I asked.

"Very high-end," Peter said. "They do custom work."

"All that you got in five seconds. If you're looking for this kind of service, you will read on. If your looking for something cheap, you won't contact them. And that is just the way they want it.

"The second thing you need to do with your website is to give people something that will make your website sticky. Let's go to www.wqis.com for an excellent example of how to make your website valuable and interesting to your target customer." At the home page, Peter and Jason saw large images of marine vessels next to the question: *Is your marine pollution insurance with WQIS?* I directed them to the third navigation link: Broker Tools.

"I want you to put yourself in the shoes of a typical insurance broker. You work with many industries, many different types of businesses. One day, you get a phone call from a barge operator. They say I operate barges that are over 3,000 gross tons, carrying oil in bulk on the East Coast. What insurance do I need?

"Now for an insurance broker, this would be quite a bit of research for the commission. But by going to the broker tools at www.wqis.com you can enter the vessel type, gross tonnage, cargo, and geography and instantly pops up the typical and optional coverages available for your customer." I demonstrated how quickly this broker tool worked.

"That's very impressive," Peter commented.

"You can print a printer-friendly version, fax it to your customer to discuss while you get a quote from WQIS for the coverage. We helped WQIS combine 30,000 data points in this database to give insurance brokers dealing in marine pollution the answers they need at the click of a mouse. We did the same thing with a State Law Directory to update all the State regulations in one source."

"How did you know to do this?" Peter asked.

"We didn't. It came out in the customer interviews during the Step One branding process. We asked brokers what would make their job easier and learned that brokers wished there was an easy way to understand what coverages were available and appropriate for their marine clients. Then, WQIS gave it to them.

"Brokers who live by this tool have a much stronger connection to WQIS, who is estimated to now write coverage for 70% of United States marine pollution insurance market."

"That's remarkable," Peter said.

"Their brand is all about leadership and they demonstrate it every day. Constantly innovating, even at their website."

"It is an initial company name though," Peter said, raising an older argument about brand names.

"This is true. They have been around since 1971 and were a quasi-governmental agency at first. Years later when more insurance players started entering the market, they found people saying things like, *My WQIS insurance is with Great American,* who was a competitor. The acronym had become so synonymous with marine pollution insurance that people thought WQIS was just the product and not the company. When their market share started to decline, The James Group worked with Richard Hobbie, III, the long-time President of WQIS, to remind people that WQIS was a company and not a type of insurance. The strategy worked brilliantly and today WQIS has five times the premium volume of its closest competitor.

"So again, Peter, you know our position on initials for companies. If you can get in a time machine and take your business back to 1971, where you are the sole business in your market for approximately a decade, then you can go with initials. Otherwise, we advise strongly against it in this new century of greater competition where it is harder to stand out."

"So what about search engine rankings?" Jason asked, "How do you achieve those?"

"That's the third thing a website has to do. A website has to be written and coded properly to achieve high organic search engine rankings. In fact, search engines are so important to winning customers inexpensively, that it has completely transformed our thinking on how to write and design websites. Now, you have to work backwards from what kind of search engine results you would like to achieve before you design.

"Let me show you. Let's do a Google search," I suggested. "Lawn Care, CT." There at the number one spot on page one of the organic search of 2.3 million listings for that search term was www.teedandbrown.com, one of our clients.

"Do another one. Let's try: branding agency nyc."

"My God," Jason exclaimed, "The James Group is number one in the organic search out of 2.1 million listings for that search. How did you do that?"

"Search ad agency nyc," I suggested. Jason found us on page one at the number 2 spot out of 39 million listings, just behind one of the largest advertising agencies in the world.

I showed him several other examples, clients that all had

page one rankings on Google. "I can't stand it anymore," Jason said. "Tell us how to do it."

"It took a few years to separate out fact from fiction for search engine rankings," I said. "But after real-world testing, and much discussion with experts in the Search Engine Optimization field, we've boiled it down to six best practices for on-site search engine optimization and four best practices for off-site search engine optimization. You have to do both. You also have to keep up with it. Unfortunately, search engine placement is something of an arms race. About 40% of your ranking will come from what you do on your site, and about 60% of the ranking comes from what you do off your website. So here's how you do it. Even though it counts less, you have to do the on-site optimization first as the basis for the off-site optimization to leverage.

"Step one for on-site web optimization is to identify the priority list of key search terms. First, you brainstorm the list of search terms your customers use to find your services. Think from your customers' perspective. Then you check those terms using a keyword tool to find which search terms are the most popular. We use SEO tools like the one our partner, Roger Wehbe, developed at www.yooter.com." I took Jason and Peter to Yooter's site and showed them the keyword tool. "This is the same as what people refer to when they say an Overature search. You enter a word like lawn care or ad agency and see how many searches are done monthly on MSN and Yahoo for that keyword or phrase. You can then export the word and search amount into a spreadsheet. Google is about twice the amount of searches for that word. So you can build a formula and add them all together and get the total of web searches per month for a given word. From this, you can prioritize which keywords you want to rank highest for.

"Step two is to adjust your website navigation and well-written body copy to reflect the key search terms you want to be ranked for. So in the case of Teed & Brown we want to say lawn care as many times as reasonable in the navigation and body copy. For example, the *Advice* button which would have brought them little in terms of searches, is expanded to *Expert Lawn Care Advice.* The James Group also specifically created a navigation link called *Choosing an Ad Agency* to help us place better for *Ad Agency* as well as help potential clients determine if we were the right fit for them."

"Can you just repeat a list of your search term again and again?" Jason asked.

"No. The search engines spiders are becoming increasingly sophisticated. Google guidelines prohibit this spam repetition technique, or hidden text, and they can actually stop including your site in the organic searches, if you don't follow their guidelines. All the other search engines tend to follow Google's guidelines, so build it first for Google and it will work for the other engines as well.

"The important thing to say about step two is all your menus and body copy that you want to rank for should be in html. No picture files. No gifs, jpgs, or flash, especially in the navigation."

"Why is that?" Jason asked.

"A search engine spider can't see pictures, only text."

"Let me show you something that will send a chill down your spine. Do a different type of Google search for your own website. Type cache:http://www.insertyourwebsitename.com. What you are seeing is the image that Google has or doesn't have of your website. Now click on the cached text-only link that Google provides. What do you see?"

"There's nothing," Jason said.

"That's because your website has been designed in flash with menus and text in pictures. Your website is invisible to the search engines."

"This isn't good," Peter said. Jason looked nervous.

"This is difficult stuff, Gentlemen." I said, "I'm embarrassed to say we didn't get great at this until the beginning of 2006, when we finally sorted out what works and what doesn't work. We've designed websites for clients in the past that don't follow these best practices for web optimization. Now that we know and you know, we both just have to do it better in the future."

"So what do we do about this," Peter said, the angry edge of his voice cut down any denial of the problem. "We can't afford to be invisible on the web."

"True. Clearly this requires action," I responded. "But you don't do anything until you figure out Step One: the Sales Moment and the Campaignable Image. Those are the handle for your brand and website. It won't take long to do it right. Then you brainstorm your sticky idea for the web. Only after those things, do you write, design, and code your website following these detailed optimization steps. Let's continue through the detailed steps, so you'll know what's involved."

"Step one of on-site search engine optimization was prioritizing your search terms so you know what keywords to use as the framework for your website. Step two was using these keywords in your navigation and well-written body copy. And of course, all these navigation links and body copy are in html text, which is the only readable format for search engines.

"But websites are of course more than just text, which brings us to Step three: use image tags with key search terms to identify photos. This turns a photo into something that can be read by a search engine spider. It doesn't score as high as actual text a person sees, but it still counts.

"Step four is to include your keywords in unique meta tags for each page. There are four kinds of tags with the title tag being the most important. The title tag is what is seen at the top of your browser. Look again at the www.teedandbrown.com home page. It doesn't say Teed & Brown at the top of the page. They know people are not searching by brand name. What does it say?"

"*Lawn Care CT, Lawn Care Service for Connecticut's Most Distinctive Homes,*" Jason said.

"It looks very reasonable to a consumer, a nice descriptor. The search engine spider zeros in on *Lawn Care CT, Lawn Care Service, Connecticut.* If someone searches those terms, and they do, the search engines know which website to give them. After backlink popularity, this title tag is given the most weight by a search engine. So it is most important that the title tags are based on essential keywords and are unique to each page. Being unique to each page in your website, helps the search engine spiders differentiate the web pages.

"The other meta tags are the title content tag and description tag which the search engines show on the search page to help you decide which link to click. Think of it as your mini ad containing as many keywords as possible in a well-written sentence a consumer would find attractive."

"What does the description tag look like for The James Group?" Jason asked.

"To tell you the truth, I don't recall," I said. "Let's do the search." In the Google organic search window on page one was: Branding Agency and Advertising Agency in NYC… Branding and advertising agency in New York City serving midsized clients nationally. Our clients make more money. Branding, Advertising, Website Design. www.thejamesgroup.com. "That first part is the meta title content tag for search engines. From a coding standpoint it is different than the topline title tag which becomes the browser page header on each web page. The second part is the description tag. It's a description of what you will find at this page."

"What's the fourth type of meta tag?" Jason asked.

"The fourth type of tag is the keyword tag, which tells search engines these are the words I want to rank for. This is where you can put your list of search terms. The thing is, all these meta tags are valuable, but not as valuable as the text seen by the user at the website. They inform the search engines what to display in searches. They score well, but they do not score as high as navigation links or body copy for rankings.

"Step five is to incorporate up-to-date copyright meta

tags for each page as search engines prefer recent content; distribution tags to let the search engine know if you should be considered globally, or by country; and robots meta tags in the code which give the search engine spider instructions to spider each page completely or skip this page."

"Why would you want a search engine spider to skip a page?" Jason asked.

"Often, you have pages that are not ready for public viewing when you are creating a site and you don't want them found until you are ready. Think about the robots meta code as an off or on switch."

"Don't all website coders know these things?" Jason asked.

I smiled gently, not sure what to say. "Ours didn't," Peter interjected.

"Step six of on-site web optimization is to create a human readable site map at your site. It also helps search engines identify links and pages to your site as well as helps users with navigation.

"The web is an interesting world. Anyone can choose 'view page source code' in their browser on any web page and see the search terms a competitor is trying to rank for. It's a constant arms race for rankings. You just have to know what the key drivers of ranking are and keep pushing them." I pulled down the view page source command on www.thejamesgroup.com and showed Peter and Jason where all our meta tags were in blue at the top of the code.

"So that's the six best practices of on-site web optimization. It will only give you about 40% of your ranking score. You have to do it because it determines what words you have a chance to rank for. Are you ready for the four best practices of off-site web optimization?" I asked.

"To tell you the truth, my head is spinning," Peter said. "We're going really fast over something I don't really understand. Jason, are you getting this?"

"A little bit," Jason replied rather hesitantly.

"I know it's a lot," I said. "We have this all written down on our website for you. And we update the best practices if search engine techniques change due to changes by the major search engines. The important thing is that you now know there is a disciplined method for creating websites that rank for organic searches and there are people like us and our SEO partner who can handle it for you.

"Should I move our discussion to Partner strategies, or would you prefer to hear about off-site web optimization?"

"I want to hear about it," Peter said. "I'm just not promising to understand it."

"Fair enough, I will do this quickly and maybe Jason can circle back with me for more detail some time. The key thing to remember about search engine rankings is they are primarily driven by the number of links to your website. This means internal navigation links on your own website, plus search engine directory links, press release links, website links and blog links.

"The first step of off-site web optimization is to build two different kinds of site maps that are read uniquely by each major search engine: a Google optimized site map, and a Yahoo optimized site map. Each have a different format, but can be easily created, then submitted to each search engine as a quick way to say, *Hello, I'm here and you should be looking at all these pages on my website.* Doing this will help the search engine spiders to find your website quicker and be more likely to index all your website's pages.

"The second step is to submit your site and keyword-laced descriptions to as many directories as possible for links to your site, called backlinks by search engines. These are your second and third tier search engines and industry directories, for example."

"The third step is issue press releases online which quickly increase backlinks to your website. They have to be written in a unique way including your key search terms in the headline and links to your website in the body copy in a way RSS readers or spiders will understand."

"Can you explain that further," Jason asked.

"For example, Juma is a superior choice for businesses wanting to do something with IP Convergence. So we try to include IP Convergence or at the least Convergence in any headline. Then we separate the web address with spaces and put the address in parenthesis. It looks a little funny in print, but it makes the link on the web and you never have to worry about the RSS readers or spiders choking on commas or periods and creating dead links that won't help." I wrote it on the board: (http://www.jumacorp.com).

"The fourth step is to purchase low-cost backlinks or get backlinks for free to increase perceived popularity by the search engines. This takes time. It's basically a PR exercise of convincing bloggers and other websites to write about you and link the appropriate keyword to your site. For example, when someone is writing about Teed & Brown in a blog, it is better they write: Looking for a lawn care company in Connecticut. I recommend Teed & Brown, lawn care, CT. And link *lawn care, CT* to the website, instead of writing: Looking for a lawn care company in Connecticut. I recommend *Teed & Brown*, linking Teed & Brown to www.teedandbrown.com. The first one scores for lawn care, CT as the search term. The second one scores for Teed & Brown as the search term. This is extremely difficult to do properly, which is why you will mostly pay people like Roger Wehbe to grease search engine wheels."

Peter looked a little queasy about this.

"I know, web backlinks is a dirty business. We didn't make the rules, we just play by them."

"Can't you just exchange links with other webmasters?" Jason said.

"We don't recommend doing this. Our search engine experts monitor the search engine forums pretty diligently. It appears that Google will be tightening its algorithms in the future to discount reciprocal links. They haven't done it yet, but it seems likely to come. Additionally, they are going to be cracking down on link farms and other black hat search engine tactics. With all their R&D money you have to bet on Google scientists. Stick with white hat approaches to backlinks.

"Quality matters most in backlinks, and this seems very fair. Every web page has a quality index score from 0-10. It's exponential, like an earthquake scale, so page rank 6 is 10-20 times more powerful than a page rank 5 depending on which search engine expert you believe. So achieving a link from www.cnn.com with page rank 8, quality index, would be worth far more than a site with a page rank 5. We check a website's page rank using Google's toolbar that you can download for free and add to your browser. Then, we know which websites to go after.

"All that being said, ranking through backlinks is primarily a numbers game since there are relatively few high ranking sites that you are likely to achieve links on. So reaching out to people and getting them to talk about your company using the right key words, is the fourth best practice of off-site web optimization.

"This is made easier when you actually have a sticky valuable idea at your website. Since link popularity is Google's number one criteria for determining the value of your website, in creating a sticky idea or application, you are also creating a reason for people to link to you. Those links will dramatically increase your search engine ranking.

"You should also pick which search term battles you want to fight. Search the term you want to rank for and write down the web addresses of the people appearing high in the search. Then, do a different type of search at Yahoo. Type link:http://www.thecompetitor'sname.com. This will display how many links a website has. If your competitor's have tens of thousands of links for a particular search term, it is going to take a long time to overtake them and you may want to prioritize other search terms."

"Alright," said Peter, "You clearly demonstrated expertise in this area. What should we be doing with our Partner strategies?"

"The biggest thing, is to have one," I said. "And oddly enough, most midsized businesses don't."

Chapter 12 Summary

Before doing business with a company, people often look at the company's website to see what they are offering, gauge the quality of the business, and see if the company is worth their time. Websites that communicate the Sales Moment and achieve high search engine rankings are essential in business today.

Websites have to accomplish three things:

1. Give people a handle, through your campaignable idea, to quickly understand your company and avoid website bounces.

2. Offer something valuable and interesting to your target audience that makes your website sticky.

3. Be written and coded using key search terms to achieve high organic search engine rankings.

40% of your ranking comes from what you do on your site, and about 60% of the ranking comes from what you do off your website. You have to do both. You also have to keep up with it. Unfortunately, search engine placement is something of an arms race.

The six best practices of on-site search engine optimization are:

1. Create keyword reports to identify the priority list of key search terms.

2. Adjust website navigation to reflect the prioritized list of keywords and include key search terms in well-written body copy that comply with website search standards.

3. Use image tags with key search terms to identify photos.

4. Include keywords in unique meta tags for each page (title tags, title content tags, description tags, and keyword tags).

5. Incorporate up-to-date copyright meta tags for each page, distribution tags, and robots meta tags in the code to tell the search engines to spider each page.

6. Create a human readable site map that helps users with navigation and search engines to identify links.

The four best practices of off-site search engine optimization are:

1. Create and submit a Google optimized site map, and a Yahoo optimized site map to the corresponding search engines.

2. Submit site and keyword-laced descriptions to as many directories as possible for links to your site (called backlinks by search engines).

3. Issue press releases with key search terms in the headlines and links in the body copy.

4. Purchase low-cost backlinks or get backlinks for free to increase perceived popularity.

Key Questions

1. Does your company website feature your campaignable idea as a handle to help prospective clients understand quickly how your website is relevant to them?

2. When you type cache: http://www.insertyourwebsitename.com in a Google search and click the cached text-only link, is your website visible to the search engines for the keywords you want to rank for?

3. Is your company website using the six best practices for on-site web optimization and the four best practices for off-site optimization?

Chapter 13

PARTNER MARKETING

"A partner is someone who believes in what you are doing and who can connect you to customers. Partners can quickly take a business to the next level," I said. "The most essential component is their belief in you. Let's talk about how to identify partners and communicate with them in a way that wins customers."

"I normally think of partners as someone who has access to my target market," Jason said.

"And what do you mean by target market?" I asked.

"The people who would benefit most from my product or service."

"Oh, I really like what you just said, *the people who would benefit most from my product or service.* That's a much better way to describe your target market. So now combine your definition of partner with your clearer definition of target market."

Jason thought for a second, then wrote the definition in his notebook. "A partner is someone who believes the people they have access to would benefit most from my product or service."

"That sounds like the basis of a partnership that will create sales to me," I said excited with Jason's clarity.

"What are you getting at exactly?" Peter asked. "Some of this is just sounding like wordplay."

"Just consider, why are there so many press release partnerships that never amount to anything?" I asked.

"I do see that a lot," Peter said.

"I think it's because neither company really believed that their customers would benefit from what the other was offering. So for your company, I want you to focus on the three parts of partnership: 1) Identifying who has access to the people who would benefit most from your product or service 2) Identifying what it will take to make them believe you will most benefit their customers 3) What's in it for them."

Jason wrote those three aspects down in his notebook. I found it interesting that Peter had stopped taking notes since Jason had come into the room. Perhaps it was unavoidable, but in my heart I knew Peter's company could really benefit from what we were discussing with Step Two tactics. I hoped he was catching the process. A CEO should understand the process in Step Two, even if he wasn't going to implement the tactics himself.

"The first two parts are the most important for successful partnerships," I continued. "People generally won't keep referring someone if it's not good for their customer and only good for them. Why?"

"Because, they will lose their customers," Jason said.

"And people will generally keep referring someone if it is

great for their customers. Why?"

"Because it makes them look good, and helps maintain a trusted relationship with the customer," said Jason. We had finally hit our rhythm, me and Jason. I felt confident I could work with him.

"A partner is also someone who doesn't compete with you," Jason added.

"That is generally true, but I deliberately recommend leaving that out. My experience is the world starts to be a different place when you look at it as a world of partners. Even companies that traditionally compete find places of synergy: through associations to raise awareness about key issues, by co-sponsoring events, or doing strategic alliances. This is the basis for so many mergers and acquisitions. Better not to rule anyone out and focus on answering who has access to the people who would benefit most from your product or service."

"So that would be step one," Jason said.

"Absolutely," I responded. "Brainstorm your list of who has access to your market."

"You mean the people who would benefit most from our product," Peter said bringing some levity to the room and rejoining the discussion.

"Good. Next to the list of potential partners, write what it would take for them to believe you will benefit their audience most."

"Well, one thing is for sure," Peter said, "if someone was going to approach our business for access to our customers, they would have to be the best in the world at what they do.

Really focused. And be able to explain it quickly, since I'm so busy."

Astonished, both Jason and I looked at Peter.

"What? What did I say?" Then Peter saw it. The reason they hadn't been successful with Partner strategies in the past. "You're saying because our brand wasn't clearly defined it made it hard for us to gain partners," Peter restated.

I pointed to him, "Actually, Peter, you said it. So you see again why Step One is so valuable: defining your Sales Moment and expressing it through a campaignable idea can help you to win partners. You see why training your people, being on message with your website and brochure is essential. All these things allow you to stand in front of a potential partner and say, *this is what we do, and why we should be doing it for people you know.*"

"What else should we explain to potential partners?" Jason asked.

"Your promise to them for how you will take care of whoever they send you?"

"Give me a concrete example, using your business," Peter insisted.

"Fair enough," I said agreeing to his challenge. "Private equity companies like to invest in mature midsized businesses. They want to see a healthy return on investment quickly to make them look smart, so they can attract more investment capital, do more deals, and make more money," I explained. "We know that good businesses don't become great businesses without perfecting brand marketing. So we say to them, *we know how to make you more money through better branding.* That's all we do. Several of our brands have become category leaders like GarageTek, Thinkfun, TransparentValue, eScholar, and WQIS. Our clients historically have grown 20-300% over three years. We've made more money than was spent on marketing for 95% of our clients. Would you like us to explain to you how we do it, with the prospect of you introducing us to some of your portfolio clients?"

"What's your Sales Moment?" Jason asked.

"We'll make you more money. If we can take a company through all three best practices of brand marketing, they have a higher likelihood of making more money. After all, well-branded companies tend to make more money than the ones that don't follow best practices."

"Sounds like I need to hear Step Three." Peter said.

"Is there anything else in it for them?" Jason asked.

"Better return on investment for their portfolio companies is the main thing. But also, deal flow. We see a lot of midsized businesses and many of them are ripe for further investment, either to take them to the next level or the owners are ready to sell. We can make introductions to the appropriate investment companies and have the credibility to get them to look at a deal immediately."

"So, are you saying you could help us get investment capital?" Peter asked.

"If appropriate. We have relationships with companies who look at smaller amounts between $1-10 million and those that are in the $25 million-150 million range.

"You don't have any relationships with firms that fill that $11-$24 million range?" Jason asked.

"Not yet," I said, "It's one of the things I would like to pursue for The James Group, but let's get back to your company.

"So to review, the first step is what?"

"Identifying who has access to the people who would benefit most from your product or service," Jason said quickly.

"And the second step?"

"Identify what it will take to make them believe you will most benefit their customers," Jason said.

"And the third is... what's in it for them," Jason and Peter said simultaneously.

"Just ask them what they would want out of a partnership. You'll be surprised sometimes by what people really want."

"What have you seen?" Peter asked.

"I've seen everything: revenue shares, commissions, please donate some money to my favorite charity, send us business, say nice things about me, to just take care of them. Every situation will be different so you have to approach them all with an open mind."

"How do you recommend prioritizing which partners are the best for you?" Jason asked.

"Prioritizing is a question of return on investment marketing, which is Step Three," I said. "So if there are no objections, let's jump to Step Three in *The Perfection of Marketing* process, Return on Investment Marketing."

"There are more things I could tell you about best practices for rolling the other tactics in Step Two: PR, Direct Mail, Print Ads, Radio, and TV, and Event Marketing, but I don't want to overwhelm you. Let's take a quick break and we can reset for Step Three.

"I have an idea," said Peter.

"What's that?" I asked.

"I'd like to bring our CFO in on the discussion of ROI Marketing. She watches our money very closely."

"I have an idea too," Jason said. "Peter, while you get Kavita, I'd like to hear what James has to say about PR."

Chapter 13 Summary

Three qualities are necessary for successful partner marketing:

1. The partner has access to the people who would most benefit from your product or service.

2. The partner believes in what you are doing.

3. There is understanding of how the partner benefits from helping you.

Of these qualities, the partner believing in what you are doing is the most important. Without this quality, you will end up with only a press release partnership.

The world starts to be a different place when you look at it as a world of partners. Even companies that traditionally compete find places of synergy through associations to raise awareness about key issues, by co-sponsoring events, or doing strategic alliances. This is the basis for many mergers and acquisitions.

Be prepared to explain your promise: how you will take care of the people they send to you and what is in it for your partner. The last part varies dramatically and should be worked out individually with each partner. Listening to what they want is most important.

Key Questions

1. Has your company brainstormed a list of companies and individuals who have access to your target market?

2. How will you have to look and act in order for these potential partners to believe you will benefit their audience the most?

3. What's in it for your partners?

Chapter 14

HOW TO GAIN QUALITY PR COVERAGE

When Peter left the room, Jason offered another confession. "We're having a lot of difficulty getting press coverage. It's one of my responsibilities, as Peter doesn't want to hire a PR agency. I've tried to tell him that connections are important, but he doesn't want to hear that. What advice would you give us?"

"How much PR experience do you have?" I asked.

"Not a lot. I know what a press release looks like. But I feel like I'm just sending them off into a void. We're not getting any interviews," Jason said.

"So it's interviews you want?"

"Absolutely," Jason said, "those lead to better quality articles."

"Very true. But go one step deeper."

"What do you mean?"

"Journalists do the interviews. They are the key to quality articles. You have to figure out how to make their lives easier."

"The journalists?"

"Absolutely. Give them a story they can easily justify to

their editors. It has to be helpful to their readers, listeners, or viewers. Then, make your company easy to interview."

"I'm still not following you."

"Here's the truth about small and midsized businesses like yours and mine: very little in our space is going to be big news, earth shattering scoops or events that will change the landscape of business." Jason nodded in agreement.

"No matter how special we think our business is," I said. "A reporter or journalist in our sphere of influence doesn't have to cover our story or any story in particular. Now think about their life and their job. They're stretched thin and under constant deadlines. There's no incentive for them to take big risks. So, they'll do exactly what you or I would do if we were in their shoes."

"What's that?" Jason asked.

"Choose the stories that are easily justified to their editors, then choose stories that look interesting to them and have a person they believe will make a good interview."

"Sure. That's what I would do," Jason said shruggingly. "So what?"

"So they're doing us a favor, by covering our companies. We have to do them a favor. Make it easy for them to do their story."

"But it's their job," Jason responded.

"Their job is to get a story, not necessarily our story. Right? So, it's our job to convince them to cover us. The best way to do that is just make it easy for them."

Jason thought for a few minutes, then opened his notebook

again. "So how should we do it?"

"You already know how to write a press release. It's the pitch you need to work on. The press release pitch has to do two things: First, explain why your business announcement is interesting to their readers and why you are contacting them. This is the quick justification they can use with the editors for why this story should be covered. Second, offer five to seven questions they can ask the key person you want interviewed."

"Shouldn't they come up with the interview questions?"

"They will. They're journalists. But including questions they can ask quickly gets them up to speed on the story, without having to do a great amount of research. It helps them quickly decide if you are worth interviewing. More importantly, it says your key person knows how to be a good interview. It shows you are a quality journalistic source that is prepared to bring something substantial to their readers and can do it quickly.

"Nearly every press release we send out has a list of questions attached, with no answers, and most importantly, how long it takes the person you want interviewed to answer the question."

"Why do you list the time?" Jason asked.

"Journalists prefer quick answers. Pithy is better."

"Can you give me an example?"

"Sure," I responded. "A journalist covering the marine community sees they can ask Rich Hobbie III, the President of the Water Quality Insurance Syndicate: *Why the Coast Guard and Marine Transportation Act of 2006 is the most significant piece of pollution legislation to affect the marine community in*

15 years? Then, the words, *takes two minutes to answer.* What are they likely to do?"

"They're reporters. They'll want to know."

"Exactly. The questions say Rich Hobbie, III is a good interview. Giving the time tells them he's prepared to give crisp answers that will be easy to insert into stories they are writing. And of course, you have to prepare and drill your potential interviewee to live up to that promise. Using this approach, WQIS continues to get in high-quality articles which support their brand position as the experienced knowledge leader for marine pollution insurance."

"O.K., I get it," Jason said, "You don't give the reporters the answers, just the questions. It gets them thinking about what kinds of things they would ask." After a few moments of silence he continued. "Isn't that using experiential marketing techniques to engage journalists? On some level, they are picturing themselves asking these questions to your client. It becomes a self-fulfilling prophecy, doesn't it? They just pick up the phone for a quick answer."

"I like how you described that interaction, very much. The questions just get the ball rolling," I said. "The key thing is we are standing in their shoes, thinking how to make things easier for them as journalists. That's the only reason it works."

"But you said, *nearly*—on nearly all our press releases. I made a note of it. When don't you do it?" Jason asked.

"We try to target our press releases to specific publications and specific reporters. In those situations, including the questions and a few sentences about why the press release is relevant to their readers is appropriate. But sometimes, you are issuing a press release for a public company. This requires simultaneous distribution to all financial disclosure points at the same time to comply with SEC guidelines. Then, you wouldn't include questions and such. But you could re-circulate the same press release to target reporters and targeted publications with questions to try to get interviews after that."

"Don't you have to have relationships in order to get stories?" Jason asked.

"I know many PR agencies say that," I responded. "But to be frank, I haven't found it to be true. The logic doesn't hold up. No matter how good a relationship is, that journalist is a professional doing a job. If it isn't a good story for their readers, they can't cover it. And if you can't make it easy for them to understand the story quickly, so they know the kinds of questions to ask, it's not going to get covered. They are busy people.

"When we contact a journalist, we tell them in the first 10 seconds why we are contacting them. Like for WQIS, we picked up the phone and said, *I am contacting you, as the editor of the Waterways Journal, with a story about changes in federal legislation that can leave U.S. marine businesses vulnerable should they not address a current gap in insurance coverage.* Their next move is simple, *tell me what you got or send it over to me.* That's it.

"We've found the most respectful thing you can do for a journalist, is not bother them, unless you have a relevant story that is valuable to them this week. There is little need for touchy-feely relationship building. They're professionals trying to make deadlines. If you don't have a story that they can use this week, don't waste their time. Using this approach, we've been successful placing the right story with the right person, even when we had never met or never worked together before.

"Of course, all this becomes much easier, when you have a consistent brand in the market that journalists recognize as doing something interesting. Then, if your lucky, they start to contact you as a resource."

Chapter 14 Summary

Many companies want to improve their PR coverage, but don't concentrate on the key to better coverage. Journalists conducting interviews are the key to quality articles.

To increase quality coverage, make journalists lives easier by including two things with your press release:

1. Five to seven questions a journalist can ask the person you want interviewed. Do not include the answer. Instead, state how many minutes or seconds it takes for your person to answer each question. Shorter is better.

2. A sentence about why you are contacting them specifically and why this story is relevant to their readers, listeners, or viewers. This shows you know that they are the right person and provides a quick way for them to justify the story to their editors.

Relationships in PR are not nearly as valuable as sending the right story, to the right person, and making it easy for a specific journalist to understand how to cover it.

Key Questions

1. When sending out press releases, do you identify specific journalists and clearly state the key reason why your story is relevant to their readers, listeners, or viewers?

2. Do you send out suggested interview questions with the time it takes to answer the questions showing you know how to be a good interview?

Step III:
Return on Investment
Marketing

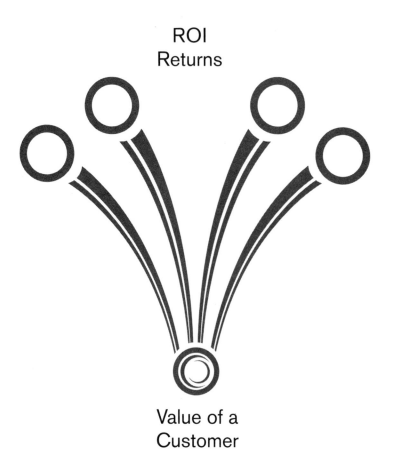

ROI
Returns

Value of a
Customer

Chapter 15

STEP III: RETURN ON INVESTMENT MARKETING

Kavita Bharati, the company's CFO, had an easy manner about her. She gave no indication of whether she was pleased to be brought into this discussion about marketing or considered it an intrusion on her day. She smiled gently. The abundance of silver streams flowing in her hair spoke to her experience and balanced approach. Looking at the CEO, Vice-President of Marketing, and CFO sitting together in the room, they presented a perfect reflection of *The Perfection of Marketing* steps.

"It's striking to have each of you here today for this conversation about your company's brand. Each of you symbolizes a crucial step in *The Perfection of Marketing* process. Peter, you as CEO are Step One: you are responsible for what your brand stands for. Jason, you as the Head of Marketing are Step Two: you are primarily responsible for consistently communicating the brand. Kavita, Peter wanted you to join us today, because you are Step Three: you make certain the company understands the value of its customer and is spending less to acquire them than their lifetime value."

"So in plainspeak," Peter said. "I'm the carrot, Jason is promoting the carrot, and Kavita is counting the carrots."

"That's good," I responded.

"More carrots is good," Kavita quipped.

"So now," I began, "Let's talk about Step Three: Return on Investment Marketing. The purpose of marketing is to make more money. We can all agree on that, yes?" Each one nodded around the table.

"If the purpose is clear, why do so few people understand how to calculate marketing return on investment?" I asked. "What I'm going to share with you now is an essential and efficient method for properly allocating marketing budgets. The first thing to understand for return on investment marketing is the lifetime value of a customer. This is your magic number. Everyone working on the sales and marketing of your company needs to know your magic number. All your management needs to know this number. You can't do return on investment marketing unless you know this magic number—what your customer is worth. You do this by running a net present value equation.

"O.K., brace yourselves," I said. "This is the moment they warned you about in high school—when algebra will save your life," borrowing a line from Val Kilmer in *Red Planet*. On the board, I wrote out the net present value equation needed to determine what a customer is worth. "It looks scary at first, but you probably know the answers to what these variables represent. We just have to fill them out."

$$NPV = \sum \frac{(\$) \, (\%)}{(1+\text{Cost of Capital})^{\text{Years}}}$$

Kavita observed the formula and nodded with her consent. She was clearly familiar with running NPVs, though I suspected like other CFOs, she hadn't considered applying them to their marketing.

"Let's get an idea what this equation can do for us. Then, we can talk about the specific value of your customer," I said. "The first number is the total revenue you get from a customer per year. You know that. We generally do a segmented NPV analysis dividing customers into small, medium, and large, but for now, think of the revenue that you get from an average customer."

"The second number is the gross profit margin expressed as a percent. You know that. Kavita, this is EBITDAM: revenue minus expenses, excluding taxes, interest, depreciation, amortization, and marketing. Kavita, why am I excluding marketing for this calculation? It's important."

Kavita smiled. "Because you are trying to assess what is appropriate to spend on acquiring a customer. Your answer needs to be before marketing expenses."

"Precisely. The revenue times gross profit margin excluding marketing is divided by your cost of capital raised to the years power." I mumbled the NPV formula quickly to get to the good stuff. "Years, is how long you tend to hold a customer and get recurring revenue from them. You know that number as well. So cost of capital is the only confusing term. It's a measure of market risk, and the company's CFO or CPA can supply that. The key thing in this equation, is cost of capital is used as a discounting factor to discount the value of a customer in order to express the answer in today's dollars."

They looked slightly bewildered, but they had made it through the hard part. Now, I could give them the payoff. "After you run this equation, you will get your magic number. Let's call it X." I wrote NPV = X on the white board. "This is the lifetime value of your customer discounted back into today's dollars. Why is it magic? Because it is the amount of profit you get to put in your pocket for a customer over their lifetime discounted back to today's dollars. After all of the salaries and overhead, all the phone calls, all the hard work, this is what you can put in your pocket."

"That's a good number to know," Peter said. "I can relate to that."

"This number will help you make powerful marketing decisions. For example, if the lifetime profit on a customer were $2,000, would you be willing to acquire them for $200?"

"Absolutely," Peter said. "And twice on Sunday. That would be an $1,800 profit."

"You would want to do it as many times as you could," Kavita added.

"Similarly," I posed, "if the lifetime profit on a customer were $500 and it took $1,000 to acquire them, would it be worth doing?"

"No, you would actually be taking money out of your pocket. And like the old joke," Peter said, "trying to make it up in volume."

"Good, you understand how to wield the value of a customer. Without this knowledge, the CEO, VP of Marketing, and CFO can't really make informed marketing decisions. You're flying blind. You can't clearly differentiate between a good marketing tactic and a bad marketing tactic. Further, knowing your magic number let's all three of you get on the same page—let's all three of you speak the language of money when talking about marketing."

They were ready to go further. "So what's your company's magic number? Let's play through the calculation for directional purposes."

I went to the white board and over the dollar sign in the NPV formula asked what the average revenue was they earned from a customer annually.

"It really ranges," said Peter. We have smaller clients that are around $20,000 a year and some of our largest accounts are nearly $400,000."

"But we don't have many of those," Jason said.

"Kavita, this is for directional purposes," Peter said. "You know how the accounts are weighted. What would you say?"

Kavita's eyes flickered back and forth as if seeing calculations in the air in front of her. "Let's go with $100,000 to be conservative."

I wrote $100K over the revenue variable. "What about gross profit margin?" I asked.

"That would be around 30%," Peter said.

"Excluding marketing dollars?" I asked.

"Still around 30%," Jason chimed in. "We're not spending much of anything on marketing."

"We're spending about 2% on marketing," Kavita said. "So let's call it 32% for directional purposes, since this is EBITDAM."

"Cost of capital," I said. "I'm guessing 15%." Kavita gave me the head bob that I had seen many times traveling in India. It meant: no worries, good enough.

"I don't understand," Peter said.

"Kavita, can you explain this one to him?"

"Cost of capital is different than the interest we're paying the bank. It's a measure of risk versus the market. The risk free amount is about 5% for Government T-Bills. Then you add the beta for how our company is performing relative to the S&P, times the market risk premium, which is the historical performance of the S&P minus the risk free amount." Both Peter and Jason stared blankly. She may as well have been speaking Sanskrit. "It's what James said, about 15%," she concluded.

"And what's the average length customers stay with you once they choose you?" I asked, taking things to a more familiar topic.

"We've had some customers since we began. They're likely to continue," Peter said. "And some for only two years. Let's call it five years." Peter looked around the room for agreement.

"Five years it is," I looked at the numbers. "This isn't a perfect calculation. I can't do a full NPV in my head, but directionally... a third of $100 is $33... minus 15% rounds to 28...times five years equals.... Your magic number is $140,000. The average lifetime value of your customer is approximately

$140,000." Kavita visualized the math again and nodded in agreement.

"That sounds about right," Peter said.

"We have a spreadsheet you can download at our website for free. Kavita can segment customers by small, medium, and large; change numbers; and assign your portfolio percentage mix and get an exact NPV number. But this is directionally sound for our discussion.

"So here's how you use this. If it took you $139,000 to win one customer, you would still be making money, and it still would be worth doing."

"What are you saying?" Peter said.

"This is discounted back to today's dollars to correlate to the moment in time when you make the marketing investment. It shows you what you could spend and still make money. Not what you should spend. *What you could spend and make money.* You have a very nice value of a customer. It demonstrates how incredibly valuable one customer is to your company and shows that you have incredible room for error in acquiring a customer." I wasn't sure they were getting this valuable principle. I needed to shift gears.

"Let's talk concretely. Let's say it cost you $30,000 to run six insertions every other month for one year in your main industry trade magazine. At the end of the year, it resulted in you winning three new customers. Was it worth doing?"

"$30,000 dollars for three customers that combined are worth $520,000. Absolutely," Peter said.

"Good. That's all you need to know about Return on

Investment Marketing. Can you win a customer for less than they are worth. As long as you are acquiring customers for less than the value of the customer, you are making money. You can evaluate every tactic based on your magic number and determine what the break even is for that tactic, then assess the risk/reward probability of that tactic. In this magazine example, you could run that same $30,000 advertising campaign for nearly five years, $150,000, before winning one customer and still break-even. So should you do it?"

"Of course," said Peter. "It's a great bet we would win many more customers if we advertised like that for five years."

"Exactly, but before we had this discussion, if I had said to you, you're going to spend $60,000 for PR this year and win only two customers, would you do it?"

"No, he wouldn't have," Jason interjected. "We even talked about something like that six months ago."

"Without understanding the value of your customer, you have no way to fairly evaluate your marketing expenses. You're flying blind. And most of the time, midsized businesses are leaving money on the table by not marketing enough. They tend to underestimate the value of their customer, so they don't spend properly on marketing, thus limiting their growth. For you, a consistent PR effort over a year is likely to bring in many more than two customers. You would make your money back in spades," I said.

"I just don't like PR. I've never spent that kind of money on PR in my life," Peter said angrily, "and I'm not about to do it now."

Many times, the very thing that management is most against doing is often the very thing that could transform the company for the better. I'd seen this over and over in my fifteen years as a brand strategist and knew to pay special attention to it. His statement couldn't be swept under the rug.

"So here it is," I said speaking with the intensity of a football coach to a team folding at halftime. "The moment where all this perfect marketing theory hits reality and falls apart. Peter, this is the moment where bad habits and personal preferences will keep us from getting to where we want to go. You've positioned the brand correctly in Step One. It was hard to do, but you did it. You rolled the brand foundation out consistently in Step Two. It took discipline, but you did it. Now, in Step Three, marketing is just math. You don't have to like it or be entertained by it. You, as the CEO, just have to understand the math. If $60,000 of PR brings two customers who are worth $140,000 each, that is a $220,000 net win after PR costs—profit spread over five years without further expense. That's not including referrals those customers could lead to, or the possibility that PR wins you more than two customers. The math says, it's a good tactic for your business. It's fundamentals. Stick to the fundamentals and you will win."

"But what if the PR doesn't win any customers?" Peter asked.

"That's why you did Step One and Step Two first. To make damn sure you have the right message and are staying on that message consistently. Under those circumstances, with your value of a customer, PR is unlikely to fail for your company, particularly using some of the techniques that I shared with Jason for PR. It's likely to put points on the board."

My intensity caught his attention. Out of desire to help, I had to be very firm from time to time with clients and even on occasions wrathful. Now I could shift gears back down to be more diplomatic. "It's true though that marketing does take time. There is always a time lag between the tactic and sales, especially when rolling out a brand for the first time. And unfortunately, some tactics do fail. To manage your marketing risk, you understand the math, then choose the tactics that will have the highest likelihood of success and the highest return on investment."

"I still don't like it," Peter said.

I took a breath to assess what to say to him. "Maybe, it's more true to say, you're not comfortable with it. I say this, because I want to help you. You say that you have never spent like that. You also never positioned the brand properly. Never rolled it out consistently. And never considered the lifetime value of your customer. These are the brand fundamentals for success—all the best practices of marketing in three steps. You don't get to cherry pick from the three steps. You have to follow all three. Otherwise, it's like a three-legged stool missing a leg. It won't stand firm. You won't make more money, and you won't become the great business you want to become."

"Well, I liked what I heard in the other two steps."

"I do too. But good businesses don't become great businesses until they use all three steps. It would be like trying to win the Superbowl with defense and offense, but no special teams. ROI marketing isn't hard. It's just new to you. Understanding the lifetime value of your customer isn't hard. And again, we have an Excel spreadsheet you can download for free at our website to help you through it."

"What do you think we should be spending in marketing?" Peter asked.

"That depends entirely on you. After you have followed the steps and understand the value of your customer, you have two choices: you can *Grow Fast* or you can *Grow Slow*."

Chapter 15 Summary

Marketing is most successful when company leadership gets involved. The CEO is responsible for what the brand stands for. The Chief Marketing Officer or Marketing Director is primarily responsible for consistently communicating the brand. The CFO makes certain management understands the value of a customer and is spending less to acquire them than their lifetime value. These company positions perfectly reflect *The Perfection of Marketing* steps.

The purpose of marketing is to make more money. To make powerful marketing decisions, company management have to understand how to do return on investment marketing, and most importantly, the lifetime value of a customer.

The lifetime value of your customer is the amount of profit the company puts in its pocket for a customer over their lifetime, discounted back to today's dollars. To calculate, use a simple Net Present Value formula (NPV). The formula looks scary, but The James Group has made it even simpler with a free downloadable spreadsheet available at: http://www.thejamesgroup.com/customervalue.

You can simply enter in designated boxes four variables and instantly understand the lifetime value of a customer. Each of these variables you are likely to already know, and being within 15% is good enough for directional purposes.

The variables to determine the lifetime value of a customer are:

1) Average annual revenue per customer.

2) Average gross profit margin before marketing expense (EBITDAM).

3) Cost of capital.

4) Average number of years a customer is held.

Without this knowledge, the CEO, Marketing Director, and CFO can't make informed marketing decisions. They are flying blind. Knowing the lifetime value of a customer allows management to clearly differentiate between a good marketing tactic and a bad marketing tactic.

Key Questions

1. Is the management team actively involved in the key marketing issues of what the brand stands for, how to communicate the brand consistently at all customer touchpoints, and how to acquire customers below their lifetime value?

2. Do the people responsible for marketing your brand understand the lifetime value of your customer?

3. Do they use this knowledge to recommend strategies and tactics that will bring your company the best return on investment?

Chapter 16

TO GROW FAST OR
TO GROW SLOW

"When rolling out a brand, a CEO has two choices," I began. Next to the customer value formula, I wrote: GROW FAST OR GROW SLOW. "You Grow Fast by creating a sizable marketing budget and sustaining it for approximately 18 months. Or you Grow Slow by choosing key strategic tactics to reinforce your sales force."

"What about dipping your toe in the water with some advertising to see how it goes?" Peter asked.

"Unfortunately, there is no such thing as dipping your toe in the water and seeing what happens," I said. "That third possibility doesn't work. Your brand will find itself with a chilly reception."

"What do you mean?" Peter asked.

"Many companies try advertising for a few months, with the strategy of waiting to see what happens. Of course, not enough will. So then they stop, wishing they hadn't flushed money away. When what they really needed was enough runway to get off the ground."

"So what do you advise?" Peter asked.

"Both strategies work. However, you have to choose your strategy ahead of time. Grow Fast or Grow Slow based on your business goals and cash position. Don't try to waffle in the middle. Don't start down the runway wondering if you have enough room to take off. Hedging doesn't work in advertising. That makes you draw the wrong conclusions, such as your brand message isn't right. When, in fact, the marketing plan is the only thing wrong.

"There is an important clue there—marketing plan. Plan implies a sustained effort over a prolonged length of time. In a cluttered world, it takes multiple touches and a sustained effort for customers to notice you, then more to change their behavior to choose you."

"So outline for me the two scenarios," Peter requested.

"In each case, you are aligning your business growth goals to your marketing budget. At The James Group, we call this part the Align Method™. In the Grow Fast case, there is a large budget invested for large growth that generally produces results in 12-18 months. The large marketing push creates a tipping point that sustains the company and brand. It's the result path. You look big and act big—just as the result will look. Perception becomes reality. In the Grow Fast case, you do all the first tactics: training people, website, brochures, partners plus a mix of larger tactics like sustained direct mail, PR, advertising, and events. I say sustained because you plan your campaign and commit to telling your story consistently for at least 12 months. Dare I say, you put your head down and just do it, knowing the results will come. Certainly you tweak the campaign as you go, but by and large you commit to 12-18 months to win your slice of the market.

In the Grow Slow case, there is a small marketing budget and smaller organic growth each year. This can go on for four to five-plus years before reaching a strong enough base to sustain the company and the brand, maybe longer. In the Grow Slow case you do all the first tactics: training people, website, brochures, partners, but you don't do substantial direct mail, PR, and advertising. You may do some, but not a substantial amount. This strategy is more about supporting the sales force. Turning every point of customer contact by the sales force into a well branded, on-message experience."

"Just to clarify," Jason said. "Why would you do some advertising in the Grow Slow scenario. Wouldn't that be dipping your toe?"

"Good question. We would recommend doing direct mail to invite key prospects to visit you at a trade show. Or putting an ad in a trade magazine encouraging people to visit you at a conference you are doing. The advertising tactics in the Grow Slow scenario support whatever activities the sales force is doing, as opposed to trying to pull sales through a well-established brand in the Grow Fast scenario.

"It's really a question of cash position and ambition. If you can invest in a marketing budget, you can create ambitious results. If you can't invest the cash, you have to expect incremental results."

"That's fair," Peter said. "But how can you predict results?"

"There is really four parts to ROI marketing and you have to model them all: understanding the lifetime value of your customer, which we went over in detail. Estimating your target acquisition cost per customer. Determining the marketing budget necessary to achieve your goals. Finally, predicting which tactics will best realize these goals."

"This sounds complicated," Peter said grimacing.

"This is really cool stuff, Peter. This is modeling your company's future to see what you'll look like and how to get there."

"Alright, continue. I'm not promising to understand it. I'm just hoping one of you two catch it," he said motioning to Jason and Kavita.

"I want each of you to understand it," I said. "It's just math. Actually, simple math at that. Let me show you.

"You have to start with some estimate of what it will take to acquire a customer. There are three ways to do this: historic, use the ad agency's prediction, and the gut check."

"I like that last one," Peter said. "Is that the scientific name for it?"

"That's better than a WAG," Jason said.

"What's a WAG?" Kavita asked?

"That's a Wild Ass Guess," Jason said.

"Historic is to look at your own historic data. Divide how much you spent in marketing last year by how many customers you gained last year. That gives you an historic customer acquisition cost. You can compare multiple years.

"Advertising agencies and media buying agencies have all

kinds of clients. Generally, they have good information on what it will take to acquire a customer, so ask them for their take on it. Then, there's the gut check. What you feel in your gut that it will cost to acquire a customer. Take that number and then double it. That's probably closer to the truth."

"So what do you do once you have that number?" Peter asked.

"We generally average all three to create the target acquisition number. Directionally, it's a good number to plan with. Every now and then, we're pretty dead on, but more likely, we're off 10-35% either way. Still, it's helpful to have a starting point to work from, then refine as you go forward."

"That's a big range for planning purposes," Jason said.

"True. But you're already way ahead of other companies by planning," I said. "Now the equation to determine the marketing budget is simple division. How much revenue you need to win, divided by revenue per customer. What does that tell you, Kavita?"

"That tells you how many customers are needed to meet the revenue goal," she said.

"Peter about how much revenue would you like to replace and then add to next year?"

"Well, through attrition we'll probably lose $2 million in revenue from existing customers. I want to get that back plus grow another $3 million."

"So if you want to replace/add $5 million in revenue and the average revenue per customer is $100,000. How many customers do you need?"

"Fifty," Peter said.

"How many customers did you win last year?"

"About a dozen," said Jason.

"And you told me you spent 2% on marketing or about $300,000. That divided by 12 is... a $25,000 acquisition price, which for your business is quite high. Let's say that we developed the brand properly. I suspect we could acquire customers closer to $12,000."

"It's really tough to win new corporate clients, James," Jason said.

"Let's plan it at a $18,000 acquisition price as an average. I'm weighting it a little toward my prediction to make the math easier." To test them I asked, "What did I say the formula was to determine the number of customers needed?"

"The amount of revenue you need to replace or add divided by average revenue per customer," said Kavita. "So in our case, 50 customers."

"Then to get the marketing budget, it's just multiplication: number of customers to acquire times target acquisition price. In your case, 50 times $18,000 is...$900,000."

"$900,000!" exclaimed Peter. "I'm telling you right now, there is no way we will spend $900,000!"

"Let's call this your Grow Fast plan then," I said. "The $5 million goal for you is achievable with this budget. But I want to show you something. What is your value of a customer?"

Peter's face went blank. He had forgotten. I pointed to the NPV number on the white board.

"$140,000." Peter said.

"What is 50 new customers times a lifetime value of $140,000."

"A whole bunch," Peter said.

"Let's do the math."

"Seven million," said Kavita.

"So let me ask it another way. Would you be willing to spend $900,000 to win $7,000,000 in profit? That's a $6,100,000 gain spread out over five years."

"I just don't like this NPV thing," Peter stated. It was as if he had just said, *I'm immune to logic*. The room fell silent.

Kavita then spoke with a serenity that surprised each of us. "James is right. It's just math. I've been with the company for five years and I haven't seen this level of clarity regarding our marketing budget. We need to change our thinking about how we approach marketing. We've been flat the last two years. I'm doing the math right now. I can see it's because we didn't budget properly to actually grow. This method is far superior to just picking a number and calling it the marketing budget. This method has a rationale. If we cannot spend that amount on marketing, then we must restate our growth targets to something that is achievable. This is preferable to being surprised and disappointed we're not growing."

Peter was clearly moved by Kavita's sincerity. "Well, James has given us a lot to think about. It's just that I'm not used to thinking like this."

"I know, Peter. It's a lot to throw at anyone at one time. But I want you to see that there is a method. There is a precise way to get to where you want to go."

"Let's say for discussion that I'm more comfortable with single-digit growth and adding only $500,000 in revenue."

"You also work up a Grow Slow plan. You still have to replace $2 million in revenue from existing clients, so $2.5 million divided by $100,000 in average revenue is 25 customers. And that times an $18,000 acquisition price is... I can't do this one in my head."

Kavita's eyes moved rapidly, visualization the calculation in mid-air again. "$450,000."

"That's more like it," Peter said. "It's just that we're losing more customers than usual this year. But I still would like to grow."

"You see what we've just done. We have aligned the growth goals to the marketing budget," I said. "Now the growth target is reasonable to achieve given the marketing budget to do it."

"Thank God!" Jason exclaimed. "I didn't see how I could win 50 customers given the current budget."

"Next," I explained, "you plan how to win 25 customers with that $450,000. You lay out your tactics and media possibilities. Analyze each tactic's reach and strategic value. Determine the cost per impression with your target customer for each tactic. Determine how many customers you have to win to break even with each tactic. And then, run a likely response rate for each tactic."

"How do you do that?" Peter asked.

"Same way. Historic response rates. Agency prediction. Gut check. For example, say historically you've won one client out of 3,000 people who see an ad in a given publication. Then, you model your ads for a .03% response rate. That allows you to predict what you can expect to gain for each tactic and of course, response rates vary from tactic to tactic. Finally, you choose the tactics that have the highest probability of success and safest break-even. Like the PR campaign we talked about earlier, where $60,000 over a year must win less than half a customer to break even. You see that is a very safe bet if first you have a well-defined brand message and a great website."

"Do you sometimes choose certain tactics to reinforce each other and work in combination to create an overall ROI?" asked Jason.

"Absolutely. That's a good insight, Jason. This goes back to the necessity for a sustained campaign. It takes multiple touches to get someone interested in your brand and more touches to push them to a sale."

"Is that true?" Peter asked.

"Sure. Has anyone in this room bought something the first time they heard about a company or product?"

"But we're different," Peter said.

"That's the thing, Peter. People are more alike than different. It doesn't matter whether we are talking about business or personal life. Every moment your mind is looking for the next thing to make you happy. But you don't just leap. You want multiple touchpoints to demonstrate that something is what you think it is."

"Give me an example," Peter said. "I'm better with examples."

"You won't even go to the movies without multiple touches. The movie industry knows this, which is why they start the movie teaser trailers sometimes eighteen months before a movie comes out and the PR buzz often when a film enters production. Then, you see the TV ads, see posters, read reviews, and even wait to hear what your friends have to say about the movie—all for something as innocuous as twenty bucks and two hours of your time."

"Well sometimes my wife and I will go see a movie, because she really likes the actor or director," Peter countered.

"Fair enough. Consider why a studio would pay more for a well-known actor or director. They want to leverage the actor's or director's brand. They know people already have multiple touchpoints with that actor or director which makes people comfortable faster. So the studio has to spend less advertising dollars to convince someone like yourself to buy a ticket. By the way, this is also a key reason why you don't want to overlook your partner marketing. Your partners have brands with many touchpoints on them that you can leverage to lower your customer acquisition cost."

"Well, how many touches do we need?"

"Typically, you have to think in terms of 6-12 touches. Your target customer has to hear and see the same message again and again from you before they believe it. They need to see a few ads, read a few articles, see you at trade shows, meet with sales people, visit your website, and talk with references or other customers. When each of these touchpoints is on brand, it creates sales. When it's not, it doesn't. Sustained consistency with the right message wins."

"You have given us quite a bit to think about," Peter said. "I can see how following these three steps would work. I want to ask about something else though. When have you failed?"

Chapter 16 Summary

When rolling out a brand, a CEO has two choices: to Grow Fast or Grow Slow. You Grow Fast by creating a sizable marketing budget and sustaining it for approximately 18 months. Or you Grow Slow by choosing key strategic tactics to reinforce the activities of your sales force.

The choice to Grow Fast or Grow Slow is based on your business goals and cash position. Don't try to waffle in the middle. You will not have enough runway to take-off and will not achieve return on your marketing investment. Hedging doesn't work in advertising. Hedging makes you draw the wrong conclusions, such as your brand message isn't right. When, in fact, the marketing plan is the only thing wrong.

In the Grow Fast case, there is a large budget invested for large growth that generally produces results in 12-18 months. You look big and act big—just as the result will look. Perception becomes reality. To Grow Fast, you do the first tactics: training people, website, brochures, partners plus a mix of larger tactics like sustained direct mail, PR, advertising, and events.

In the Grow Slow case, there is a small marketing budget and smaller organic growth each year. This can go on for four to five-plus years before reaching a strong enough base to sustain the company and the brand, maybe longer. In the Grow Slow case, you do the first tactics: training people, website, brochures, partners, but you don't do substantial direct mail, PR, and advertising. This strategy is about supporting the sales force: turning every point of sales force customer contact into a well-branded, on-message experience.

There are four parts to ROI marketing and you have to model them all: 1) Understanding the lifetime value of your customer (Chapter 15), 2) Estimating your target acquisition cost per customer, 3) Determining the marketing budget necessary to achieve your goals, 4) Predicting which tactics will best realize these goals.

There are three ways to estimate your target acquisition cost per customer: 1) Historic, 2) Use the Ad Agency's Prediction, 3) The Gut Check. It is best to use all three methods and compare or average your results for planning.

The equation to determine your marketing budget is simple. Marketing budget = (target revenue ÷ average customer revenue) x target acquisition price.

This method's rationale is far superior to just picking a number and calling it the marketing budget. If you cannot spend the amount on marketing necessary to achieve goals, it is better to restate your growth targets to something achievable.

Determining how many customers you have to win to break even with each tactic, and then, running a likely response rate for each tactic, are the keys to choosing ROI-appropriate marketing tactics.

Business people that understand the math of ROI marketing are superior at strengthening and growing businesses. ROI Marketing is particularly powerful for small and midsized businesses that can't afford to waste money. It is essential to not only manage your costs, but not leave money on the table.

Key Questions

1. Did your company make a clear decision to Grow Fast or Grow Slow and then back it with the appropriate marketing plan?

2. Have you seen much success in marketing from companies who dip their toe in the water and see what happens?

3. Is your company correlating customer acquisition cost to company revenue targets in order to create the marketing budget?

4. Is your company modeling response rates and break even rates to determine the lowest risk/highest reward marketing tactics?

Chapter 17

WHY THE PERFECTION OF MARKETING WORKS

Peter's question echoed in my mind: *When have you failed?* It was time to tell them about the secret step in *The Perfection of Marketing* process—the key factor that makes all these techniques work.

"To fail in marketing is to make less money for your client than what they spent with you," I said. "To be certain, it has happened. Each time, I feel sick about it. I agonize about what I could have done better and how to prevent it from happening in the future." Peter, Jason, and Kavita's silence signaled they wanted me to go further into our failures.

"*The Perfection of Marketing* process was developed to solve an ethical quandry. *How could anyone consistently create marketing success? How could we take money from clients and know we would bring them more in return?*"

"Very good questions," Peter said solemnly.

"These questions drove me to contemplate and distill the essence of successful branding, advertising, management, finance, and even philosophy. I realized that these were more than business questions—they were life questions. I looked for and found best practices. I saw clearly how to boil these practices down into practical steps that actually could be implemented by time constrained and resource strapped businesses. Approaching from a consistency perspective created *The Perfection of Marketing*—all the best practices of marketing in three logical steps. As we discussed earlier, you position the brand, roll it out consistently, and use the lifetime value of your customer to guide marketing expenditures."

"To be fair, there are lots of steps and procedures under each of those three steps. You've explained a lot of detail today," Peter said.

"True. Lots of opportunity for failure, which is why we have to be disciplined and keep using best practices at each stage of the process."

"So when do you fail?" Peter asked again.

"This gets to the key factor in *The Perfection of Marketing* process. All these techniques work because they come out of the one and only best practice."

"Tell me more," said Peter, waiting for me to reveal the one and only best practice.

"You see, there are really two parts to your question. I've thought a great deal about this. There's *when* do you fail? And *why* did you fail? And the two answers are very different."

"The *when* is the easiest to admit. Having made more money for 95% of our clients and lost money for 5% of our clients over 12 years of work, the pattern is easy to diagnose. The *when* occurred, when best practices weren't followed.

Shortcuts were taken due to the client budget, rushed timing, or some of the best practices skipped, even out of laziness. Sometimes, we get away with skipping a step. But in each of the cases where we didn't make more money for a client, I know exactly which best practice was skipped and it came back to bite us."

"Which practices get skipped?" Jason asked.

"The practices that get skipped have been in three main areas. The first is skipping customer interviews because the client doesn't want you to talk to their customers, or they don't want to pay for the research, or it's a start-up business and there aren't any customers to talk to. This leads to not identifying the Sales Moment sharply enough to convert sales consistently. Without being certain of the mental image that makes target customers buy, it's very difficult.

"We've learned from our mistakes and know better how to overcome them. For businesses with customers, you just can't skip talking to customers. It gives tremendous, invaluable insight to identify their Sales Moment. For start-up businesses, you need a different strategy. Some of our greatest marketing successes have been with start-up companies. However, nearly all our marketing failures have come with start-up companies. If you eliminate start-up companies, The James Group success rate over the past 12 years is around 98%.

"With start-ups, it's much harder to predict if the market really wants their product and what the actual Sales Moment will be. So now we're very careful about what start-up businesses we take on. They have to have a very robust business plan, do more market feasibility testing, and it's best to have a lengthy cash runway to tell the story for a year, so adjustments can be made in the light of real market feedback."

"What's the second best practice that gets skipped?" Jason asked.

"Creating the employee brand book and following on with training. The problem for companies that don't do this is their brand discipline frequently goes out the window and management starts to try new crazy things that are simply off brand because they didn't understand the brand; didn't understand how important consistent messaging would be to their success; or sometimes, they're just bored.

"We try to overcome this by appealing to a company's long-term thinking and stressing the benefits of internal branding. Though sometimes, we have to circle back and implement it later, once the brand gets off-track and management realizes they now have an internal problem."

"And the third?" Peter asked. "You said there was three."

"You could probably guess. It's skipping ROI marketing," I said. "Some clients don't want to take the time to understand the value of their customer or how to use it. It's hard. It's a new skill."

"It was a little confusing for me at first, because I'm not used to thinking about marketing as a measurable investment," Peter said, "but I know Kavita understood it. In general, I agree with the concept."

"That's a good start," I responded. "But the most predictable mistake is not planning and not sticking with a strategy to

Grow Slow or *Grow Fast.* Both clients and sometimes even we try to hedge. Again, that doesn't work."

"What specifically was your single worst failure?" Peter asked.

"My single worst marketing failure was with a mortgage company launch. The brand was perfect, the rollout foundation near perfect, but the ROI launch was botched. The marketing budget was initially planned for $4 million over 18 months. Management started to make some strategic business moves with their operations and kept trimming the marketing budget again and again. By the time of brand launch the budget was $300,000 for an eight-week test. It was complete marketing hubris to think that eight weeks could launch a brand in the crowded mortgage market. I said as much, but I didn't stop it by not participating. I wanted to believe the brand was strong enough to generate a quick start. I was wrong. The campaign didn't make a dent and it proved to be poorly spent money. It was my worst marketing failure."

"Did any good come out of it?" Jason asked.

"Sure, from the test, the company did discover a niche in FHA loans for first-time homebuyers and that was a great benefit. But in truth, that eight-week test was money poorly spent, and a mistake that should have been avoided. Fortunately, we remain friends. We later had the opportunity to help them with some Grow Slow tactics."

Kavita interjected, "You said there were two parts to the question. The when do you fail and the why. So why did it fail?"

"The why can be summed up best by the Buddhist Master Shantideva. His name means Angel of Peace. He said:

All the happiness in the world
Comes from taking care of others.
All the suffering in the world
Comes from taking care of yourself.

Peter, Jason, and Kavita sensed the truth of those words.

"The why is harder to admit. We've failed when we put the interests of our business first, over the client. When the motivation to help others is no longer pure. It's self-concern, rather than a sincere desire to use our talents to solve a client's problem.

"We've also failed when the client put their personal likes or comfort level ahead of best practices. And to be fair, that second failure is still ours, because try as we do, sometimes we've been ineffective in persuading clients from doing something we know is going to be unsuccessful."

"How did you know?" Peter asked.

"Because it wasn't following the one and only best practice of putting the customer first," I said. "It had little likelihood of working."

"So you see, why something fails has two flavors, but they are both from the same root—*taking care of myself first.* It's self-cherishing: a desire to protect myself first. The pressures of business are tough. I get concerned with how we are going to make payroll, rent, taxes, or even grow. That's when I'm going to make a mistake. I might hold back with clients, because I'm afraid we will lose the account or project if we don't do exactly what they want. There is always room for collaboration and compromise, but when we know something breaks brand best practices and will lead to future pain for a client, it's better to take the pain now and address it.

"To overcome this tendency to protect myself, I stand in their shoes. *What would I do if this were my business?* It takes my natural tendency to be selfish and makes me selfish standing in their shoes working for their happiness. Then, the motivation stays pure, and the real branding and marketing insight flows. This is how to apply Master Shantideva's teaching to marketing and it works spectacularly."

"That has to be hard to do," Jason said.

"It's really just a new habit. It requires discipline. *Am I thinking about them or thinking about me?* Once you recognize the pattern: that you're exceptionally helpful when you are thinking about someone else and bad things happen when you're thinking first about yourself—then, it becomes an easier habit to adopt.

"You see, The James Group is at its best when we forget about our own business. When each person on the team exchanges themselves with the client, stands in their shoes and thinks *what would I do if this were my business and everyone was depending on me to get it right?* We ask ourselves this question continuously when developing strategies and creative. It's a very powerful question that sets a proper motivation helping us to forget about our own selfish needs or even design tastes. Thinking about the client first is the core of our culture and success. Everyone at The James Group knows it is better to tell the truth and risk losing a client, than implement something comfortable we know won't work. We build this commitment to the client from the beginning in our contracts: if what we're doing isn't making them more money, a client can cancel us at any time. We make it easy for them. They don't pay for work they don't want."

"How do you get past the client judging things based on what they like?" Jason asked.

"The second flavor of why we fail is equally difficult to squash. And this is the client that puts their personal likes or comfort level ahead of the customer. We try to guard against this one by helping the client to see that the test isn't what they like. It's thinking from the customer's perspective. It's following best practices. It's what performs for the customer in the marketplace. These are the tests. For branding and advertising, their customer is more important than they are. After all, how much of your own product can you really buy?"

"Not enough," said Peter. "We need more customers."

"Clients succeed when they stand in their customers shoes: talk how they talk, see what they see, think how they think. Clients who communicate to their customer in the way that the customer prefers, do great. Making things easy for customers to understand is really a form of kindness.

"Occasionally, we hear from clients: *but I don't like it. It's my company. I don't want to look like that*. We have to gently remind them: *but do your customers like it? Do your customers*

want you to look like that? So we help clients to guard against
the most common client mistake: talking to themselves, which
is a kind of self-cherishing, forgetting to see the world from
their customer's perspective."

"You're really just talking about good customer service. The
customer is always right," Peter said.

"I guess I am," I said. "But it's more than that, isn't it?
Motivation to help others first is the final, secret step in
The Perfection of Marketing."

"How so?" Peter asked.

"You see, a *Perfection* is something done with wisdom and
compassion at its core. I've seen business people struggle with
their marketing, so I've brought all the best practices together
into three logical steps that any business can follow. This makes
marketing easy for them. Now, you clearly understand how
marketing works and can follow these steps from beginning
to end to produce remarkable results. This is compassion. I
don't want to see you or any other business people suffer from
avoidable marketing mistakes.

"And, if what Master Shantideva says is true—*all the
happiness in the world comes from taking care of others*—that
wisdom recognizes you can't experience something good
yourself, until you first give something good to others. Now this
is a very deep wisdom. It's difficult to see and hard to do. It has
taken me years of daily meditation and testing like a scientist in
my daily life to appreciate how important continuous intention
to help others is to making anything work, including marketing
practices.

"In fact, every mistake I have ever seen occur in business or life always boils down to one root thing: we're you thinking about yourself first or other people first."

"Are you suggesting that we meditate to make our marketing better?" Peter asked.

"Do what works for you. I personally think many people would benefit from meditating. But rather than attempt to convince others of the wisdom driving each point of *The Perfection of Marketing* process, I've built the method into each of the marketing techniques. This way, even without seeing the truth of why things fail or succeed for yourself in meditation, the intention to serve the customers first will be strong as you implement these techniques. Putting customers first is the one and only reason why these marketing techniques continually work."

"Can you show us what you mean exactly?" Peter asked.

"Let's look back at *The Perfection of Marketing* process knowing what you know now. To position the brand, we were thinking about the customer's unmet mental image—their Sales Moment. Then communicating their Sales Moment through brand name, logo, tagline, and campaignable image. Were we thinking about us?"

"No," Peter responded. "We were thinking about them."

"Exactly, we were thinking what would make it easier for another person to make a purchasing decision in a cluttered, chaotic world. And that is a form of kindness. Simply, making their life easier.

"In rolling out the brand consistently, we made sure we

lived up to our promise at every touchpoint. For the benefit of the customer, we trained our people to deliver on the brand consistently. We even provided an easy campaignable handle at our website so the customer could quickly determine if we are relevant to them. Further, the search engine optimization was done using the words and language the customer uses to search for what they want. When Jason and I spoke about PR, it was all about how to make the reporters' lives easier."

"That's all true," Jason said.

"When we talked about Return on Investment Marketing, it was in the context of honoring how valuable each customer actually is. That's why we started with the lifetime value of a customer. It was tricky for us, but acknowledges our customer is extremely valuable. We don't have to be cheap in inviting them to buy from our company. They are worth it. We can maintain a generous spirit as we go about our marketing. Through simple cause and effect, by being generous, we will experience a world that is generous to us."

"But aren't we doing these best practices to make more money for us?" Peter countered.

"Absolutely. No contradiction," I said. "Motivation to put the customers first is why you will make more money. It's why our clients have consistenly made more money for over 12 years. Their customer gets exactly what they want. The client gets exactly what they want. More happiness in the world. More happiness for everyone. Everyone wins.

"Peter, Jason and Kavita, I want to see you get exactly what you want by helping others first. What I have said to you today with all these practices is simple. Put your customer first. Don't think about yourself. Think about what your customer wants to see, hear, and what they want you to look like. Make it easier for that person to make a choice in a crowed, busy, chaotic world. They have so many other pressures in their life. Be what their heart desires most.

"Do that. Do it consistently. And you will achieve *The Perfection of Marketing*."

Chapter 17 Summary

The Perfection of Marketing process was developed to create consistent results.

Marketing efforts fail more often when a marketing best practice step is skipped. This is how it failed. However, this is not why things fail. The why things fail reflects a deeper wisdom. *All the suffering in the world comes from taking care of yourself first. All the happiness is the world comes from taking care of others first.*

Marketing tends to fail when the advertising agency puts its needs in front of the client or the client puts their needs in front of the customer. In fact, every mistake that occurs in business or life always boils down to one thing: were you thinking about yourself first or other people first.

The antidote is to exchange yourself with others. Stand in your customers' shoes. Think about what the customer wants to see, hear, and what they want your brand to look like. Think how to make it easier for them to choose this brand in a crowded, busy, chaotic world. Intention to help the customer first is the one and only factor that makes all these marketing tactics work.

Key Questions

1. Has your company skipped any steps in the *Perfection of Marketing* process?

2. Are you happier when you are helping others or helping yourself?

3. What would make it easier for your customers to choose your brand?

ABOUT THE AUTHOR

James Connor is the CEO and founder of The James Group, a brand strategy and full-service advertising agency in New York City serving midsize business clients nationally. Over 12 years, James has honed The Perfection of Marketing process and overseen the creation of over 70 brands including category leaders GarageTek, Thinkfun, TransparentValue, and WQIS. He is well regarded as a speaker on brand marketing. James meditates daily and in the evening teaches Buddhist philosophy for the Asian Classics Institute primarily in New York City and the Hamptons.

For four-color visual examples of the work discussed in Step I, Step II, and Step III, visit: www.PerfectionofMarketing.com. For assistance developing your company's brand, communicating your brand consistently, or with ROI marketing, contact The James Group at 212-243-2022 or visit www.thejamesgroup.com.

Our clients make more money.™